The Diagnosis and Treatment of
Intimate Relationships

How to assess the wellness of your relationship:
Key indicators and steps to restore it to health

RICHARD JOHNSON

Ark House Press
arkhousepress.com

© 2025 RICHARD JOHNSON

All rights reserved. Apart from any fair dealing for the purpose of study, research, criticism, or review, as permitted under the Copyright Act, no part may be reproduced by any process without written permission.

Cataloguing in Publication Data:
Title: The Diagnosis and Treatment of Intimate Relationships
ISBN: 978-1-7642308-5-8 (pbk)
Subjects: FAM029000   FAMILY & RELATIONSHIPS / Love & Romance; FAM030000 FAMILY & RELATIONSHIPS / Marriage & Long-Term Relationships; REL012030 RELIGION / Christian Living / Family & Relationships.
Design by initiateagency.com

Disclaimer
All names, identifying details, and personal information used throughout this book have been changed to protect the privacy and confidentiality of individuals. Any resemblance to actual persons, living or deceased, is purely coincidental.

ACKNOWLEDGEMENTS

I would like to express my gratitude to the numerous relationship counsellors, therapists, authors, and elders who have paved the way for us in our profession. A special acknowledgment is due to Nicholas Benjamin and the team of staff from the UnitingCare Qld Family Relationship Centre. The reflections shared in this edition likely draw from the multitude of case meetings, insightful client experiences, and the emotional challenges we face as mediators.

CONTENTS

Acknowledgements.. iii
Prologue..vii
Foreword...ix
Introduction – *Taking Your Pulse* xi

1 Foetal Heart-Beat – *Coming Together*................................... 1
2 Preventative Health Care - *Appreciating your differences* 7
3 Differential Diagnosis - *Negotiating your differences* 12
4 Cardiac Arrythmia – *Clumsy communication and conflict*...... 25
5 Congestive Cardiac Failure - *Sharing Responsibilities*....... 40
6 Cardiomyopathy – *The build-up of tension*........................... 49
7 Coronary heart disease – *Loss of Passion*............................ 57
8 Hole in the Heart – *The missing pieces* 70
9 Cardiac Embolus – *Maintaining boundaries* 77
10 Heart Transplant Donor - *Relocating* 103
11 Pericarditis – *Finances and property*................................. 109
12 Stab wound to the Heart - *Betrayal* 116
13 Cardiac (Myocardial) Infarction – *The death of a child*..... 125
14 Congestive Cardiac Failure – *Co-dependency* 132
15 Autoimmune Diseases – *Self-destroying your relationship* ... 138
16 Turning off the Life-Support – *Ending a relationship* 147

17 Athlete's Heart – *Long-term and mature relationships* 161
18 Cardiologist – *Relationship counselling/therapy* 168
19 Respiratory System – *Replenishing love* 173

Appendix – *Long distance relationships* 177
Bibliography 183

PROLOGUE

The first edition of this book, titled *Pulsating Love,* originated from my desire to share heartfelt wisdom with my youngest son as a wedding gift. He was embarking on the journey of marriage. Previously, my two older children had entered into marriages that unfortunately ended in separation shortly thereafter. This prompted me to reflect on how the success I have experienced in my professional capacity as a relationship therapist, coupled with my own long-term intimate relationship, did not naturally extend to my children.

One day, my daughter provided me with an insightful observation. She remarked, "We were positioned to fail. On the surface, you and Mum appeared to be free from conflict and difficulties in your relationship, and as children, we never learned how to react when circumstances became challenging."

To prevent my youngest son from facing similar challenges, *Pulsating Love* was created as an effort to provide him and his new spouse with a valuable gift—the life lessons and knowledge that have supported and fostered the success of my 40-year relationship.

Five years later, my younger son is thriving in his marriage, and my older children appear confident and content in their current relationships.

Over the past five years, I have undertaken the challenging task of assisting separated couples as they work to navigate their futures independently.

These futures are often complicated by factors such as children, jointly owned property, and a history of intense conflict, hurt, betrayal, and grief. It has become evident to me almost daily that the outcomes for many of the individuals I work with could have been significantly different had they learned and applied the wisdom and principles contained in this book. Most notably is the 'transactional' premiss from which many couples attempt to build a robust intimate relationship, only to realise that when the going gets tough such a foundation is shifting and shallow.

From the outset, and in an attitude of transparency, the guiding premises on which this book is based are a desire, a willingness, and a commitment from both parties to build their relationship on a rock-solid foundation of sacrificial giving and sacrificial forgiving.

This second edition, titled *The Diagnosis and Treatment of Long-term Intimate Relationships,* is enriched with real-life anecdotes, and shaped by the experiences of over 500 couples. It is my hope that you will find value in the non-clinical, non-academic style of this book for yourself or someone you care about.

FOREWORD

In a moment of insight and curiosity the famous singer-songwriter, Buddy Holly, enquired of his own heartbeat: –

Heartbeat, why do you miss when my baby kisses me ...?
Heartbeat, why do you skip when my baby's lips meet mine...?

From the romantic times of antiquity, through the pragmatic times of enlightenment, to the sentimental present, the heart has played a central role in the fortunes of the world. The heart has been the source and cause of grand adventure and tragic demise of many a brave and foolish soul. *Love, so the lover says, is as strong as death, its passions as fierce as the grave, it bursts into flame and burns like a raging fire.*[1] And, with this pulsing, pounding heart we have all experienced a rush of blood.

From the moment Richard asks you to find your pulse, and to feel your pulse, he is inviting you to come to yourself and to examine your relationship with others through your own heart.

Go on. Put your finger on your pulse. Better still, allow someone else to feel your pulse, and notice when it skips a beat. Is it arrhythmia or is it love?

---

[1] Paraphrase from the Song of Solomon 8.6

Richard personally and imaginatively draws on his experiences and skills as a nurse, a counsellor, a therapist, a man, a husband, a lover. Just like taking an ECG, Richard traces the rhythms of our relationships. Rising and falling with each beat, breathing, and sighing as the pressures flutter, we can feint or burst in a moment.

Sometimes the relationship dynamics he tackles can be sobering indeed. Each chapter addresses a critical care issue for our hearts and for our relationships. With careful insight Richard then offers practical resources and treatments that are honest and heartening.

Now, if the thought of a heart attack unnerves you, maybe the thought of heart massage may just be the most intimate and vulnerable of desires. To place your heart into another's hands is a profound act of trust, to hold another's heart is a terrifying privilege. The only way is through an open heart.

Because the heart is such a complex and mysterious organ it requires specialist care and attention.

Why, then should our relationship be deserving of anything less?

Now, take your pulse again.

I heartily commend *Pulsating Love* and *The Diagnosis and Treatment of Intimate Relationships* from one whom I know whose own heart seeks only what is good, and true and noble for all our hearts.

Rev James Stevenson
Minister Uniting Church in Australia.

INTRODUCTION – TAKING YOUR PULSE

Your pulse is your heart rate, or the number of times your heart beats in one minute. Pulse rates vary from person to person and are lower when you are at rest, and increases when you exercise, get excited, and when more oxygen-rich blood is needed throughout your body.

THE DIAGNOSIS AND TREATMENT OF INTIMATE RELATIONSHIPS

Before proceeding further with this book, can I encourage you to take a moment to check your pulse. You can do this by placing your fingers on the inside of your wrist near the thumb, or on the side of your neck. Lightly move your fingers until you feel the rhythmic beating of your heart.

Checking your pulse is a straightforward method to remind yourself of the necessity for active care in both your physical health and your intimate relationships. Whether at home, in your vehicle, or awaiting an appointment with a therapist, taking a moment to feel your pulse can serve as a reminder of the importance of regularly monitoring the health of your intimate relationship.

Over the years, both physical health and relationships have encountered numerous challenges. Cardiovascular disease remains the leading cause of mortality globally, and divorce rates have increased by over 250% since the 1960s. Cardiology focuses on maintaining heart, health and early detection of related issues, employing treatments ranging from medication to surgical interventions. Just as active measures and, at times, medical treatments are necessary for the physical health of your heart, relationships benefit from self-reflection, diagnosis, and, at times, intentional action to enhance their health and happiness.

This book draws parallels between maintaining heart health and ensuring the well-being of relationships, using common heart conditions as metaphors

Extensive research has been conducted on relationships, resulting in numerous academic papers and self-help books. However, these resources can be frustrating if they don't speak to your own situation, or they are not readily available when assistance is required.

INTRODUCTION – TAKING YOUR PULSE

This book draws parallels between maintaining heart health and ensuring the well-being of relationships, using common heart conditions as metaphors. For example, assessing whether a relationship has a strong rhythmic beat, experiences chronic congestive failure, suffers from narrowed coronary arteries, is in cardiac arrest or maybe it has an autoimmune disease.

Often efforts to enhance relationship quality are comparable to administering first aid to a chronic heart condition. Performing Cardiopulmonary Resuscitation (CPR) is appropriate during cardiac arrest. However, if an individual requires open-heart surgery or daily medication, it would be imprudent to rely solely on CPR skills as the primary strategy. Conversely, one might fear that only extreme measures, such as open-heart surgery or a heart transplant are the available options and not realise that substantial improvements can be achieved through guided lifestyle modifications or non-invasive treatments.

Many individuals struggle to maintain a lifestyle conducive to heart health. Observations made during a visit to a shopping mall will reveal the difficulties people have in managing a healthy weight, due to dietary choices, exercise levels, or underlying medical conditions. Similarly, readers may struggle with their energy levels, optimism, and/or their desire to invest further efforts in sustaining a healthy and fulfilling relationship.

Readers are encouraged to take their time reading each chapter of this book, thoughtfully considering the state of their relationship. Even if the described dynamics do not perfectly align with their own experiences, recognising similar conditions in others can enhance personal growth within their own relationship. The intention is to foster awareness rather than direct intervention.

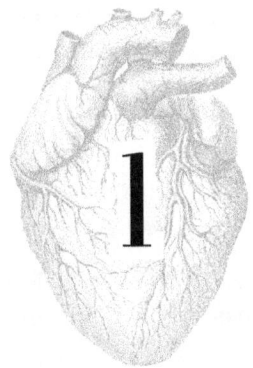

Foetal Heart-Beat – Coming Together

Hearing a baby's heartbeat for the first time is an exciting moment for new parents-to-be. A foetal heartbeat may first be detected by a vaginal ultrasound as early as 5½ to six weeks after gestation – sometimes sooner and sometimes later. The average foetal heart rate is between 110 and 160 beats per minute and changes as your baby responds to conditions in the uterus.

No matter the current state of your relationship—be it thriving, requiring improvement, in a chronic state of disrepair, or seemingly lifeless—it is undeniable that the relationship began at some point.

Reflect on the early stages of your relationship when your pulse was likely to be elevated with excitement. Take a moment to pause and recall those memories. Consider the first time you encountered your partner, or perhaps it was not the initial meeting but rather the first time you truly noticed them.

Can you recall the specific attributes that stood out to you? Perhaps it was their attractive appearance, their distinctive mannerisms, or their unique sense of humour. Alternatively, it might have been the profound sensation you experienced when you realised they were checking you out in a manner unlike anyone else had before. What emotions did you experience at that moment? What are your current feelings? How would you describe the state of your relationship today? Is it still robust, healthy, and bringing a subtle smile to your face and a sparkle to your eyes? Or is it experiencing irregularities? Have your memories faded, leading you to question whether your relationship is approaching a point of stagnation?

Romantic Love

I have observed in numerous discussions and publications that individuals often either misinterpret the significance and influence of romantic love within their relationships, or they minimise its importance to such a degree that it is nearly deemed inconsequential to the durability of a relationship.

Romantic love is often associated with strong, fast, and palpitating pulses. However, just as it is not healthy to experience constant tachycardia and palpitations, it is not necessary to continuously feel romantic love to maintain a strong and healthy relationship.

It is noteworthy that individuals who are considering separation often express that they are no longer 'in love' with their partner. While their feelings are genuine and valid, the interpretation they assign to their experience typically pertains to romantic love. They may not feel the same level of attraction as they did during the initial stages of their relationship, and it is common for them to cease engaging in romantic activities together. Sexual intimacy may have diminished in intensity or become infrequent or non-existent. Declaring a lack of love can be likened to stating that their emotional connection has ceased. It might be more precise to assert that the romance in their relationship has waned—akin to a weakening pulse. Despite the weakened or imperceptible pulse of the relationship, it does not necessarily imply that the relationship is beyond revival.

> *Despite the weakened or imperceptible pulse of the relationship, it does not necessarily imply that the relationship is beyond revival*

People are affected differently by the language they use to describe the health of their relationships. The word 'love' is used to convey various meanings by different individuals, and sometimes even by the same individual in different contexts. For instance: I love my partner, I love my mother, I love my children, I love my dog, I love my neighbours, I love my job, I love my beer, etc. Several languages, such as Greek, Italian, French, Latin, have multiple words that more accurately define and communicate the nuances of relationships, whereas English primarily uses the word 'love'. In Greek:

Eros: Sexual desire or passionate love. Eros was the Greek God of love and sexual desire.

Philia: Friendship.
Ludus: Playful friendship (between Philia and Eros).
Pragma: Longstanding commitment.
Agape: Universal love of humankind, altruism, and sacrifice.
Philautia: Love of the self.
Storge: Love within the family (parents, siblings, children, etc.).

If you're an average punter like me, using the Greek language is not something that readily comes to mind, but that's not the point. When individuals consider the state of their relationship using phrases like "I am in love", "I am no longer in love," or "I found the love of my life," it may be beneficial to put aside the word love and explore language that more precisely describes their experience. Refrain from using the love word and, for example, say to yourself, "I really like the way that person looks at me and laughs when I tell a joke," or "that person frequently criticises the way I do things around the house."

Similar to which words you use, the narratives or metaphors people use when referring to the health of their intimate relationship can be either helpful or unhelpful. Be careful when describing love as something metaphysical such as 'the merging of halves', or perhaps as something kinaesthetic such as a 'protective dome' or 'fluid-filled bubble' where the two of your souls reside. Many of these narratives originate from Hollywood productions or Mills & Boon novels.

Whatever language, narrative, or metaphor an individual or couple may use to understand and communicate the state of their relationship, it is important to recognise that language and narrative are only conceptualising tools, and they may pre-empt, or powerfully influence the direction of your intimacy. Where possible, avoid black and white language or narratives. For example, we're either in or we're out. Metaphors that offer flexibility are more helpful, such as ties with varying degrees of strength, or distance with varying degrees of closeness.

Importantly, if the metaphor you are using is not helpful in managing the health of your relationship, either to enhance your togetherness or facilitate your release, you can replace it with something more effective.

Returning to romantic love, it is important to acknowledge the significance of romantic love in all relationships, even those that are long-standing. Minimising or invalidating its importance is an error in judgement. Romantic love is both influential and essential. It not only initiates our contact with our partners, but also serves as a reminder of the heartfelt commitments made at the beginning of the relationship throughout the months and years, including during trials and hardships. Just as an embryo's heart begins its rhythmic action in a miraculous moment, and though our hearts often function without our conscious awareness for most of our lives, they continue to perform a crucial role. Romance plays an integral part in healthy relationships. As with all efforts to maintain a strong and healthy relationship, attention to romance is important.

> **Romance plays an integral part in healthy relationships.**

Try this exercise: while taking your pulse, recall the activities you engaged in with your partner at the beginning of the relationship—such as romantic gestures, activities, conversations, places you visited, etc. Most of these actions were likely not spontaneous; rather, you and/or your partner made intentional decisions and took some personal risks.

You might not be able to replicate the specifics of your earlier experiences together, but it's beneficial to consider what you can plan together and take some risks to emphasise the importance of romantic love. Currently, if you feel comfortable doing so, set aside the deep analysis and diagnosis of your relationship, focus on the present moment, and explore ways to reintroduce romance into your relationship.

Case History

My first case history is about my own experience with romantic love. I vividly remember knocking on a fellow university student's door for newspapers for a sociology assignment. She opened the door, and her smile, youthful skin, and sparkling blue eyes caught my attention. 40 odd years later, three adult children, four grandchildren, and one great-grandchild (crikey I'm sounding old) my heart still races at that memory. Each Saturday morning, my wife and I enjoy breakfast together, laughing through the trivia quiz and crossword in the local newspaper. Perhaps the writing of this book is the ultimate sociology assignment I was given so many years ago.

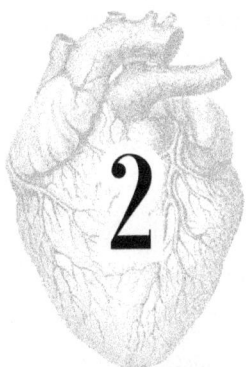

Preventative Health Care - Appreciating your differences

Preventive healthcare consists of measures taken for disease prevention, as opposed to disease treatment. It includes routine health care such as screenings, examinations, tests, check-ups, and patient counselling to prevent illnesses, disease, or other health problems. The purpose of preventative health care for your heart is to reduce the risk of heart disease and to identify problems early on so that action can be taken to keep your heart from becoming more seriously ill.

The thing about taking your pulse is that it is one of the easiest and least intrusive methods of monitoring your everyday heart rate. Let's look at a few of the more common experiences and see how these can also help to focus on the health of your relationships.

Firstly, there is the speed of your heart contractions – that is, the number of beats you would feel when you time your pulse for a minute. Obviously, the rate of your heartbeat varies depending on the context of your immediate experience. If you are racing to catch a bus or working out at the gym, your heart rate will be much faster than if you were, say, lounging by the seaside reading a novel.

At the inception of your relationship, when romantic love dominates and you are enchanted with each other, we can assume your pulse was racing - both literally and metaphorically. As a couple representing each chamber of your heart you were in synchrony with each other and coordinating well to ensure the propulsion of blood flow through your body was life giving.

Generally, in the early stages of a relationship partners tend to be more aware of their similarities with each other and somewhat blinded to their differences. The speed and the acceleration of your level of intimacy is high when you are experiencing moments of romantic love, and in the early stages of a relationship partners are aligned and they enjoy the mutual experience of a rapid pulse rate.

> *In the early stages of a relationship partners tend to be more aware of their similarities and somewhat blinded to their differences*

Herein lies one of the first dangers in managing the health of your heart and the health of your relationship. It is neither realistic nor healthy to experience a continuously racing heart rate beat – tachycardia – and it is unrealistic to expect both partners to have the same beating action. In a healthy heart the different chambers don't beat together, they beat in rhythm and in synchrony. Albeit people might accept that living continuously in romantic love is unreasonable, they may still hold on deeply, and unconsciously, to the belief and the expectation that to be in-love with your partner is to be the same as your partner.

Relationship issues tend to arise when differences emerge between each partner's perceptions and expectations of the strength and pace of your relationship's heart. As you start to notice differences in your partner, you may realise that some things will tend to arouse your own [literal] heart rate while they are having little impact on your partner.

> *Relationship issues tend to arise when differences emerge between each partners perceptions and expectations*

A common and very delicate time is when you notice the differences in the speed and acceleration in the level of intimacy in the relationship. Although the development of intimacy does take place during times when you are together sharing intense experiences – both positive and negative – it also develops over many years of steadily living your lives together. Often one partner might desire to maintain the momentum of their racing heartbeat, while the other might be more subdued or even experience an unusually slow heat beat – 'bradycardia'.

The partner desiring a more rapid pace might voice something like, "Our relationship is not going anywhere" or "He/she doesn't seem to want our relationship to go to the next level." They might consider introducing activities to fire-up the relationship, perhaps engage together in new experiences, and/or create a crisis.

The time of differentiation between partners is also when the question of compatibility is likely to come into one's thoughts and into conversation. It is during this time of enquiry you will need to explore each other's deeper beliefs and values. Surface level similarities on the things you like, and those you dislike, make wonderful ingredients for romantic love, but they will struggle to sustain your relationship when times get tough. Partners who have a close alignment in their beliefs and values are better equipped to negotiate their aspirations and outcomes for their lives and for their partnership and are more readily able to resolve their immediate conflicts.

> *Partners who have a close alignment in their beliefs and values are better equipped to negotiate their aspirations and outcomes*

The contrary also applies where a couple have significant differences in their beliefs and values it is highly likely that they will experience many more incidents of disagreement.

Regardless of whether a couple's beliefs and values are in close alignment with each other, as they move into a phase of differentiation anxieties associated with attachment and separation may begin to emerge or intensify.

I'm going to change metaphors for a moment. Imagine you were looking to buy a house. You come across one for sale. It isn't perfect, but it seems to be just right for you - right size, good location, and in solid condition. You feel good about it. Then, when you ask about the price, you find out that it's way, way too expensive. Ah!! But you also discover that you may borrow all that you need to purchase the house. All good so far. The downside, however, is that you will need to spend the rest of your life paying off the loan. In addition, because of the size and schedule of the repayments you are required to make, you will never have enough money to buy anything for enjoyment. Week by week, month by month, year by year, you will only ever be able to afford the basics for keeping yourself alive.

What are your options? 1) bite the bullet, borrow the money, purchase the house and hope that your work promotion comes up sooner rather than later; 2) walk away and keep looking at other houses; or 3) negotiate a price for the house that you can better afford.

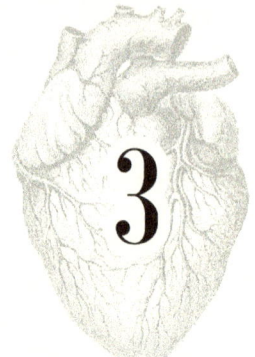

Differential Diagnosis - Negotiating your differences

A doctor asks incisive questions, listens carefully, and runs tests to understand what's really going on with a person's heart. Negotiating joint decisions when intimate couples have differences in beliefs, values, opinions and habits also requires an intentional effort to understand each other's position, their needs and fears. A doctor will consider multiple possible causes before choosing a treatment plan and intimate couples would do well to explore multiple options and creative solutions before settling on a final agreement.

DIFFERENTIAL DIAGNOSIS - NEGOTIATING YOUR DIFFERENCES

The unilateral desire for a partner to go to a deeper level of intimacy, or a deeper level of commitment, or even the reality that some of the things that arouse your partner (positively or negatively) are different from your own, can be quite challenging. At this stage, regardless of whether you are deciding to persevere in your discomfort, preparing to compromise on your expectations, or whether you want your relationship to end, one thing is for sure, you need to be able to negotiate with your partner.

Negotiation plays an essential role in the preventative health of your relationship

Just like romantic engagements, negotiation plays an essential role in the preventative health of your relationship. As your relationship matures, it becomes clearer that you are both still individuals, with your own sets of beliefs, values, dreams, etc and you need to negotiate your own personal relationship boundaries. You can't expect each other to be mind-readers or to simply assume that you agree with every eventuality. This might have been your experience when you were first caught up in the romance of your coming together, but sooner or later your respective individualities will re-surface and you need to be able to work out your differences. And yet negotiation skills within an intimate relationship are one of the least developed skills couples demonstrate in the management of their relationship.

Just as a good diet and regular exercise are essential for minimising the risk and maintaining the health of your heart, negotiation requires knowledge and training, practice, and discipline. Partners who are competent in negotiating the differences they bring to their relationship are like marathon runners who have disciplined their training to ensure their heart rate matches the stage of the race.

When it comes to the preventative health of your relationship, we can consider your regular romantic engagements with your intimate partner as the physical exercise required to maintain a healthy heart - your daily walk, cycling or workout at the gym. Negotiation on the other hand, is a bit like a balanced diet. Each day and many times a day we consume meals, snacks, and beverages to stave off hunger pangs and to keep ourselves healthy. Similarly, negotiation that is in an intimate relationship is pervasive in our daily lives. We negotiate trivial matters such as who is going to do the dishes tonight, who do we invite for dinner on the weekend, or what to watch on TV, etc, etc. At other times we regularly negotiate more important issues such as whether to have another child, where will the kids go to school; the make of a new car; accepting a new job, relocation and the amount of money we should borrow.

Competency in negotiation is essential and vital in intimate relationships. It's a skill, it's not a talent. You need to learn how to negotiate with a balance of power, with a willingness to sacrifice, and with diplomacy. No-one (well at least most people) do not like being dominated or controlled by another person, and indeed even the fear of being dominated can lead to unhelpful defensive strategies when negotiating.

These days my work mainly involves mediating with separated couples to resolve their disputes with parenting arrangements and property splits. Countless times I wonder to myself whether their situation could have been avoided if only they had been able to negotiate their difference much further up-stream, before so much water had gone under the bridge and before they went over the falls and now the relationship has ended on the rocks.

Notwithstanding the need to deliberately learn and develop the skills of negotiation, effective negotiation in a relationship doesn't require us to have advanced training in international conflict or the release of hostages in a siege, though I would imagine that sometimes it might feel that way[2].

There are five components to effective negotiations: 1) being clear about what you both want to achieve – your high-level mutual goal; 2) laying-out or listing any and all the possibilities for reaching, or at least would be heading you towards the goal; 3) take turns, considering, exploring and testing of your respective preferred options; 4) be future focused, making note and putting aside the niggling, usually unresolved issues that serve as 'rabbit holes' that attempt to distract you – in other words stay on task; and 5) always be respectful in your communications and look for every opportunity to complement your partner – even if they seem unwilling to budge. Acknowledge and intentionally give voice to the strengths that you recognise in each other.

1) **Define the mutual outcomes** that you both want to achieve, or in other words, *set the agenda*. This is possibly the most difficult and most important part of the negotiation process. It is during this time that your stated beliefs and values will be reaffirmed, and/or they will be tested for their authenticity. If you are not able to agree on your mutual goal you may need to chunk it up to a higher level. For example, let's say you want to negotiate whether to visit your mother for her birthday or go to a barbeque with your partners friends. Before you start putting voicing your respective opinions, ask yourselves what it is that is mutually important to you both. It might be, say, that it is important to you both to make the best use of your limited recreational time on the weekend, or that it's

---

[2] Where issues of conflict involve potential separation, parenting, safety and/or intimate partner violence please consult with a professional counselling and/or family mediation service.

important to you both to strengthen and/or support your friends and family. You might have differing opinions (visit mum or go to your partner's barbecue) on how you might fulfil these mutual goals, but you have at least commenced your conversation by affirming your togetherness. At first it might sound a little trite, a waste of time or you might think that it doesn't help to resolve your actual dilemma, but strangely it helps to soften your own and your partners rigid opinions on what they consider the best option. Try it out. I am not kidding. Many couples come unstuck because they overly focus on, intensify, and give priority to the route to take over the more mutually important destination. Whether you end-up negotiating an amicable parting of your ways or looking to resolve a difficult area of conflict, coming to an agreement on what you hope to achieve from the negotiation enables a deeper understanding of each other and creates clarity in your purpose. A typical starting point is for a couple to negotiate the division of their free time and disposable finances into three categories – 1. the portion for *ME;* 2. the portion for *WE*; and 3. the portion for *FAMILY* or *OTHERS*. The mutual higher order goal is for fairness and equity in the relationship. The pathway to achieving this is where you need to refine your negotiation skills.

> *Coming to an agreement on what you hope to achieve from the negotiation enables a deeper understanding of each other and creates clarity in your purpose*

Note 1: *It is important not to rush ahead and start proposing options for resolving the issues until the desired outcomes for both partners are clearly articulated and agreed on. Most conflicts are not* *so much about the desired outcomes, but more about how and by what means each partner believes is the best approach to take to achieve the best outcomes.*

Note 2: *If neither you nor your partner are considering separation, it is a good practice to clearly state this up front and make it clear that dissolving the relationship is not on the agenda and is not to be used as a negotiation strategy to coerce one partner towards surrendering to the other partner's position.*

> **Most conflicts are not so much about the desired outcomes, but more about how and by what means each partner believes is the best approach to take to achieve the outcomes.**

2) Individually **laying out or listing all the options,** the possible means and methods for reaching the mutually important, higher-level goal. This is classically called a *brainstorm session,* where you allow your thoughts to flow freely and creatively with the possibilities. List them in three categories:
   o *Category 1*: options in which you have no emotional investment or determined position.
   o *Category 2*: those for which are not negotiable, and you will not consider at any time.
   o *Category 3*: proposals that you would consider with certain conditions, or with trade-offs.

The above process applies even if your list turns out to be a dilemma with two mutually exclusive options. That is, we either do this or we do that, but we can't do both. In the example above, going to your partner's barbecue might fall in category 3 and generally we might be willing trade off with some other conditions such as leaving early before the football comes on TV, but because my mum has stage 4 cancer and likely to die in the next few days it is leaning a lot towards category 2.

Let me crank this up. Hypothetically, you would like to accept a promotion in your company and relocate to a town where you hardly know anyone; your partner, however, wants you to stay in a routine job in a community where you are well settled with family and friends. Your mutual and most important goal is not to separate nor attempt to have a long-distance relationship. How would you categorise your respective positions? A word of caution: the more determined you are that your position is non-negotiable the more likely your mutual goal will become under threat.

3) **Prioritise and Discuss Each Option:** The hard work comes as you review and discuss each other's lists.

Items listed in *Category 1* are usually discussed reasonably freely and without too much angst. They are no big deal and probably just required you both to articulate and clarify the details regarding the when, where, how and who of the item.

For items in *Category 2*, however, we need to spend a bit more time discussing these. Items that you might be regarding as non-negotiable are to be considered very seriously. You may be surprised at how much agreement you have with your high-level non-negotiables as often the items listed in Category 2 resonate with the core values that drew you together originally. For example, you may agree that maintaining the relationship itself is a non-negotiable, as also is the safety and health of your children, or not engaging in criminal activity, taking illicit drugs, and the like.

DIFFERENTIAL DIAGNOSIS - NEGOTIATING YOUR DIFFERENCES

For other items you might be considering as non-negotiable you will need to weigh up whether you are prepared to sacrifice your higher-level goal if your position is not agreeable with your partner. As such, it is important that you diligently prepare your points for consideration. You need to have a sense of certainty in your position and be very, very clear as to your rationale for this certainty. You need to know, not merely feel, precisely why it is critically important to you and more importantly that you are confident that you can present your position in such a way as to persuade your partner to genuinely agree with you.

I say genuinely because you don't want your partner to agree with you simply because you have stated that "this is non-negotiable." A dynamic such as this is fundamentally a strategic misuse of power. Your partner would be conceding to your position, not because they genuinely believe it is the best option, but because they hear these words as a veiled threat. A threat that you will abandon your mutually agreed high-level goal(s) unless your method or preferences are followed. Of course, if this indeed is your or your partner's strategy you may need to consider whether there is a power imbalance in your relationship.

If you do reach an impasse with non-negotiables, you will need to go back, revisit and review your intended high-level goal(s). You both will need to consider how important the issue is to the health of your relationship. To quote someone (probably a movie character) is this worth "dying in a ditch" over. Make no mistake, however, a significant impasse that cannot be resolved, or is resolved only by compromising the core beliefs of one or both partners, is a red flag for incompatibility, and sooner or later the health of your heart will deteriorate.

In short, a position of non-negotiable is never to be taken lightly and is best reserved for the big-ticket issues where you already know you are in agreement with your partner.

Now, for the more time-consuming *Category 3* items. This is where the hard work, and indeed the most satisfying work, happens. It's the untold conversations that arise every day, every week, and every year of your relationship. This is where you can live being different from your partner and yet indelibly, organically, and spiritually connected to your partner. In keeping with the food metaphor, this is where the chewing, swallowing, regurgitating, dieting, and fasting takes place. It is where the compromises and trade-offs occur.

Some people often refer to this as a balancing of the wants and needs of each partner. Unfortunately, the word *balance* tends to conjure up an image of two pans connected with an oscillating pivot, as if there were only two things that require consideration to reach a point of equilibrium. Or for those who are more numerically oriented, a score card of wins and losses.

When a couple engages in negotiation there are multiple and often complex wants, needs, fears and uncertainties that need to be weighed up and considered. The hope is not for an end result where you each get your fair share of wins and losses, but to come away affirmed that your partner (not you) is the primary focus of your love and that your relationship is strong and sustainable.

As you negotiate the items in Category 3, you both need to clearly articulate what makes each item (from both your lists) significantly important to you individually and on your relationship, and what you believe could potentially happen if the item(s) were to be compromised.

The key words here are 'potentially happen'. Rather than assuming you and/or your partner can predict the future, give yourselves scope to consider other possible impacts and eventualities – greater or lesser – on either/or both partners, and on the relationship.

Think laterally and creatively. Ask yourselves if there is anything you might be overlooking or missing in your deliberations. If you find you and your partner are in polarity, is there a middle ground? Try changing the context surrounding the items of difference (dare I say dispute). Could the issue(s) of difference and/or your proposed options for addressing your differences gain or lose some of their validity if they were considered in the frame of a different culture, a different time period, by a different age cohort, or people from a different socio-economic background. Any shift in context might help to get a new perspective on your issue(s). Sometimes a way forward in a negotiation can be reached when one or both partners put aside their sense of immediacy. An agreement could be made between partners to park the issue for the time being and return to it at a determined later date when you have more information or when the context of the issue might have changed.

You would be naïve to think that negotiating your *category 3* items is always reasonable and void of emotion. Of course not. At times we can be very passionate about the issues that are important to us, and our communication shortcuts may veer towards disrespectful. If you notice yourself and/or your partner emotionally escalating you may need to call time-out and structure your communications (see chapter 4, titled 'Cardiomyopathy' for structured communication) to ensure you are clear in expressing your respective wants, needs, and fears, and you are also clear in understanding those of your partner.

4) **Stay on task** and don't be distracted by concerns that seem to resurface from past issues[3]. Invariably words are said in conversations that trigger memories, emotions and automatic responses which serve only to send you down a rabbit hole and distract you from reaching a negotiated outcome.

---

[3] I heard where a couple were able to resolve a niggling (odour) issue by installing a door between their ensuite bathroom and their bedroom.

These unresolved issues are very real, very powerful, and loaded with hurt and resentment. You need to be able to recognise when they come to the surface in your more difficult conversations. Agree to temporarily park them and agree to deal with them another time.

So, let's imagine now is the time to deal with this thing once and for all. Well firstly, you are kidding yourself if you think you can simply forgive and forget. Albeit you might be able to drive a stake into the heart of this intruding ghost from the past, but by no means is it likely to never surface again. Taking time to deal with them means deciding together how you will manage them each time they do arise.

The key to resolving niggling issues is a paradox. That is, you resolve them by not trying to resolve them. You listen to what the other person is seeking to express from their experience. Don't argue, rationalise, or reason with them, just listen, and listen some more. Be curious and ask questions that might help you to understand the issue. If you can't understand why someone did what they did or find a way to make sense of their decisions at the time, or you become confused by what is said, be prepared to sit and accept that somethings are not available to be understood at this time. If you can identify and tune in to each other's feelings, do so, and then enquire about what it would take to be able to move forward from, or live with, the issue even if there were to be no clear resolution – acknowledge, appreciate, apologise.

Situations can and do change, however. Life goes on and people develop and mature. If you find yourselves getting stuck in the mud of the past, after acknowledging that the past was difficult and hurtful, ask each other these two simple questions: 1. "If that was the situation then, what is it like now?" And 2. "How do we want things to be different in the future?"

If you are courageous and willing to take a risk together, give the issue a cute name and apply an equally appropriate remedy to it. For example, it could be a known fact that one partner made a clumsy decision in the past that cost the relationship a significant amount of money. In the heat of negotiations this niggling issue often emerges and takes the conversation down a well-worn rabbit hole. You know you can't change the past so having listened to the real feelings of disappointment, resentment, guilt, or whatever, refer to the incident as, say, 'the ugly scarecrow' and metaphorically spike it and sit it silently in a paddock somewhere.

Case History

George had an extramarital affair 45 years ago. Both he and his wife were aware of the affair, but he never acknowledged it openly and he never apologised. From time to time when he and his wife needed to negotiate a difficult issue and she found herself struggling to be heard she would throw in some form of reference to the affair – the 'Big A'. One evening when this happened in the presence of friends, one who happened to be a police officer. George went into his typical rage and threatened to shoot his wife. Consequently, he had his firearms confiscated and a Domestic Violence Protection Order was issued. On the Order it stated that George needed to attend an anger management course. It was there that he had his epiphany. Finally, after 45 years he made time to sit with his wife and discuss what happened in the past. He apologises, not only for what he did 45 years ago, but also for all the angry outburst he went into over the years whenever the issue emerged. Occasionally the 'Big A' still yells out in his wife's thoughts and now she simply quietens it in her mind and is better positioned to stay on task in difficult conversations.

5) **Wrap-up with genuine compliments.** Compliments are an acknowledgement of the strengths and qualities in your partner. If you find it difficult you can start by simply expressing your appreciation and respect for the other person for being willing to engage with you to find an acceptable outcome.

Now, if you are anything like me, you would have read through this section fairly quickly and might have thought to yourself, "Yeah, that makes sense, I need to be up-front about my wants, needs and expectations, and set some clear boundaries to protect my interests." Yes! Yes! Yes and No!

Yes 1: you need to be comfortable and confident to articulate your thoughts, ideas, opinions, beliefs and feelings about the things that are important to you.

Yes 2: you need to work with your partner to discern a higher-level position of agreement between you both before you argue your respective individual differences.

Yes 3: you need to consider that there are possibly three pathways to achieve the desired future with your partner — your way, their way, and the better way.

And

No: negotiation is not about protecting your self-interests. It's about developing a strong, secure and loving relationship that will transcend anything and everything that life is likely to catapult at you.

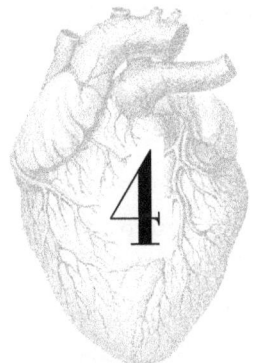

Cardiac Arrythmia – Clumsy communication and conflict

When you feel your pulse, it feels like a single thump as your heart contracts to propel the blood flow throughout your circulatory system. In fact, each pulse you feel is a sequence of very well coordinated micro-contractions between the various chambers of your heart – between your right and left atriums and ventricles.

When your heart is healthy and functioning well in sinus rhythm, the contractions between your heart chambers are in perfect synchrony and allows the blood to move through each chamber, firstly through to your lungs to release carbon dioxide and receive fresh oxygen, then back to your heart to distribute oxygen rich blood throughout the body. As you can imagine, if the sequence of your heart's micro-contractions loses their synchrony, the movement and efficiency of blood flow throughout your entire body is affected.

It is quite common in every relationship, no matter how long a couple has been together or how mature they are, for one or both partners to feel out-of-sync with the other. This could happen in almost an infinite number of different contexts – from how you prefer to use your time, spend your money, discipline your children, contact with your parents, colours of your rooms, what to prepare for dinner, what to watch on TV, etc.

At the more extreme end of being out-of-sync with your partner you might begin to experience a sense of alienation from them. You might start to wonder whether your partner cares about you at all. Or you entertain the possibility that they might be having an affair. Most tragically, in preparation for the impending hurt and rejection that you imagine is about to unfold you might then choose to protect yourself and take steps to withdraw from your partner and look elsewhere to invest your loving endeavours. You guessed it: in response to your behaviours your partner reciprocates your fears and what commenced as a little out-of-sync turns into full-blown cardiac fibrillation.

Although skilful negotiation will help you to manage the more significant differences you have in your life expectations, maintaining the daily synchrony in your relationship requires constant and effective communication as well as deliberate, self-sustaining, intimate and exclusive rituals.

Maintaining the daily synchrony in your relationship requires constant and effective communication

Interpersonal communication is not something you need to develop from scratch. Like cardiac arrythmia, it's not as if your heart has stopped beating; rather it could be doing much better in its job of keeping you alive and well. Let's face it, if you have managed to make a connection with your partner and have started on a relationship journey together you must be doing something right. However, no matter how wonderful you think you might be at communicating, the effectiveness of your communication is solely measured by the impact it is having on your partner[4].

Rather than assuming you have any communication deficits, let's focus on some things you can do to restore and maintain synchrony with your partner.

Daily Health Supplements

Remembering to take regular health supplements has never been my strength. I always reach a point of forgetting to take the vitamin tablet or I simply lose faith in whether it is having any beneficial effect. When my level of self-discipline falls dismally short, I rely on various reminders to keep me on track. Three routine interventions that I have found easy to remember and which have greatly assisted in developing and maintaining a healthy sinus rhythm in a relationship are: eating breakfast together when you wake each morning, reconnecting immediately when you both return home each day, and retiring to bed together at the end of the day.

1. Breakfast together: of course, this doesn't need to be a full cooked breakfast or even a bowl of cereal. A simple cup of tea or coffee could be enough, or nothing at all if that's your thing. It's about having a little us-time, and it might only be for a few minutes, to synchronise yourselves before you get carried off into your daily activities. You could talk about how you both slept, any dreams you may have had, what you have on your respective schedules for the day, or any reminders you need to give each other. You might

---

[4] Of course, if you're anything like me, I reckon my partner has some difficulties picking up on the wonderful wisdom that I have to impart.

also consider doing a short devotional reading together if that resonates with your beliefs/culture, and/or telling each other that you love each other.

2. Reconnecting: this activity needs to happen immediately you and your partner come back together having been otherwise engaged throughout the day. Even if you have kids hounding you for your attention, let them wait, and spend the first precious moments together alone with your partner. Each day, you and your partner experience untold individual events, conversations and thoughts which might not seem like a big deal over a short time, but each moment away from each other you are changing, albeit very slightly. Over a longer period, the changes you each adopt into your personality may become more noticeable and significant. Spending time alone, perhaps going for a short walk, when you come back together each day gives you an opportunity to share your individual experiences of the day and it helps to keep you in synchrony with any changes happening within each other.

3. Bedtime: go to bed together. Synchrony in your relationship extends even into your times of intimacy and there is nothing more intimate than going to bed together. Whether this leads to sexual intimacy or not is irrelevant. Retiring to bed together is a very strong demonstration to your partner and to any others in your household, that at the end of the day, when it's all been said and done, the most important person in your life is your partner.

> *When it's all been said and done, the most important person in your life is your partner*

Other daily strategies could be a daily walk together, going to the gym together, doing a daily crossword together, reading/watching and discussing the daily news, having a pre-dinner drink together, cooking the evening meal together. Whatever activity appeals to you the two key words are 'daily' and 'together'.

Pace-maker

Damage to the heart due to ageing or some diseases can affect its ability to set the correct pace for your heartbeat. Such damage can result in slower than normal heartbeats or long pauses between heartbeats. The damage to the heart can also cause it to switch erratically between slow and fast rhythms. A pacemaker is a small device that's placed in the chest or abdomen to help control abnormal heart rhythms. This device uses electrical pulses to prompt the heart to beat at a normal rate.

As your relationship develops and matures. it will, without a doubt, experience some rough and turbulent times. Like your heart, your relationship inevitably ages, and for some people it can become tired and easily fatigued. Being disciplined with your preventative strategies and taking your daily health supplements, as prescribed above, will certainly reduce your risk of damage and deterioration of your relationship but there may come a time when some more intensive intervention is required.

- Regular date nights: many couples have introduced regular date nights into their weekly, fortnightly, or monthly schedules to deliberately plan for quality time together. The pace-making

The pace-maker effect is significantly dampened if you simply follow a routine over-and-over again

impact of date nights is achieved mainly because they are regular, and the activity or event is planned in advance. Don't leave it to spontaneity or 'playing it by ear' on the night. Likewise, to maximise the benefit of the date night it needs to have variety. Although the time spent together is more important than the actual activity or event itself, it is important that whatever you plan to do together it includes novelty and new experiences.

- The pace-maker effect is significantly dampened if you simply follow a routine over-and-over again – e.g. going to the same old club/restaurant for dinner each week. It can become boring and before you know it you find yourself sitting together, no conversation, perhaps staring at whatever is happening in the environment, or reading the latest post on your device. We'll cover more on this when it comes to unblocking your 'coronary arteries'.

My wife and I have made it a weekly event to have a special breakfast together each Saturday morning. Rather than the routine bowl of cereal and pot of tea, we try to prepare something different – e.g. avocado smash, bacon and eggs, muffins, expresso coffee, or whatever else we can try out from a breakfast recipe book. As well as doing the crossword in the local weekly news magazine we might discuss family, politics, current affairs, spirituality, you name it - especially when the caffeine from the coffee kicks in.

- Take a break (from each other): scheduling time away from your partner, either alone or with others, allows you to stay in-touch with your individuality and strengthens your ability to contribute to the health of your relationship. Some people might achieve this by going to work at a site other than where your partner is working, and/or participating in a sporting activity without your partner. Other people plan a weekend away or have extended holidays without their partners.

Note 3: *There is one very strong caution with this pace-maker intervention – in everything you do during your time away from your partner, maintain a mindful awareness as if your partner is present with you. Taking a break from your partner is never a license to breach your fidelity or confidence with your partner– verbally, physically, or otherwise.*

Case History

Peter was experiencing increasing difficulty connecting emotionally with his wife. He felt emotionally barren in comparison with her vibrancy. He wondered whether he was experiencing depression, but rather than going to the doctor and being prescribed antidepressants, he took a week off work and went fishing in a remote area of the rainforest. He told me that after a few days alone and before he was about to return home, he was sitting in his boat in the middle of the river. It started to rain. He was wearing his raincoat and broad-brimmed hat. There was no wind, and he said that he wasn't cold. He told me that an overwhelming and deep feeling of loneliness came upon him. As the rain poured over him, he said that thoughts of his wife flooded his mind and pined that she would be with him. He said that for the first time since as far back as he could remember, he started to cry, and cry, and cry. He described his experience as an emotional awakening. And to the point of this case history, he said that when he returned home to be with his wife, he felt like he was really coming home. He was back in sinus rhythm.

Defibrillation

One of the most serious abnormal conditions of the heart is fibrillation – very rapid irregular contractions of the muscle fibres of the heart resulting in a lack of synchronism of the heart action. The most serious form of fibrillation is a cardiac arrest when the heart suddenly ceases to function. When a person experiences cardiac arrest, it is critical to their life to stop the fibrillation of the heart by administering a controlled electric shock and adrenaline to restore the heart to sinus rhythm.

Conflict in a relationship is inevitable and natural. There is no wisdom at all in trying to avoid conflict or pretend that the absence of conflict is a sign of a healthy relationship. There are times, however, when the conflict between partners may reach such a high level of intensity (fibrillation) where thoughts of ending the relationship start to emerge and may threaten the end of the life of the relationship.

> *Conflict in a relationship is inevitable and natural. There is no wisdom at all in trying to avoid conflict or pretend that the absence of conflict is a sign of a healthy relationship*

> **Note 4**: As you are running to grab and apply the defibrillator strategies listed below – don't put voice to any thoughts of divorce, separation or dissolving the relationship. If these are genuine possibilities then they can be discussed with your partner later and

CARDIAC ARRYTHMIA – CLUMSY COMMUNICATION AND CONFLICT

hopefully with the assistance of a professional relationship counsellor/ therapist.

Strategically located in the hospital setting are what are commonly referred to as the crash cart. It's a trolley of specifically preprepared drugs and equipment, such as a defibrillator, intravenous equipment, intubation tube, etc. When an alarm is raised that a person's heart has gone into cardiac arrest, the crash cart is set for action.

> **Note 5**: *Before conflict arises, you and your partner need to discuss the defibrillating strategies you will apply in the event of an emotionally intense conflict and agree that should either partner initiate the defibrillation strategies, you will both comply even if the other partner doesn't feel like it's necessary at the time.*

Attempting to resolve conflict during times of intense emotion turmoil is futile

Attempting to resolve conflict during times of intense emotional turmoil is futile and highly unlikely to lead to a satisfactory outcome for either partner. In times of conflict when you become aware that you seem to be moving further and further away from finding a resolution, take a mindful moment to check-in with yourself: your level of emotional intensity, the volume of your voice, the speed of your conversation, your breathing rate, the tension in your body, especially around your neck and arms fidgeting, arm waving or other movements. If you're sufficiently mindful, give yourself a score on a 1-10 rating scale and ask yourself if you need to call time out. If you are not able to rate yourself, then you have already reached a point to call for a break in the conversation.

In calling for time out, always agree with your partner that you will return to the issue(s) and, if possible, determine the duration of time out.

For example, you might agree to talk about the issue(s) tomorrow morning when you are not so tired, or when any alcohol has worn off. You might simply take 15 minutes to cool off, perhaps go for a short walk or make a cup of tea for you both, or you might agree to make time to meet with your relationship counsellor/therapist.

As well as affording you space to de-escalate your emotions and body tensions, time-out also provides you with the opportunity to understanding the dynamics of your conflict. Diagram 1 depicts the interactive cycle that gathers momentum during times of interpersonal conflict with your partner. Understanding and applying the cycle to specific times of conflict can help you to short-circuit the conflict and return you to sinus rhythm (regular heartbeat).

> *Always agree with your partner that you will return to the issue(s) and, if possible, determine the duration of time out*

Cycles of conflict generally have their basis in the way each person is viewing and interpreting the behaviour of their partner (including what is being said by their partner). A person will filter their experiences depending on their beliefs, values, personal history, and projected expectations. The cycle might start with an action (or unexpected inaction), behaviour and/or comment, from one person.

Following it through with Diagram 1, let's pick it up with Partner A on the left-hand side of the cycle:

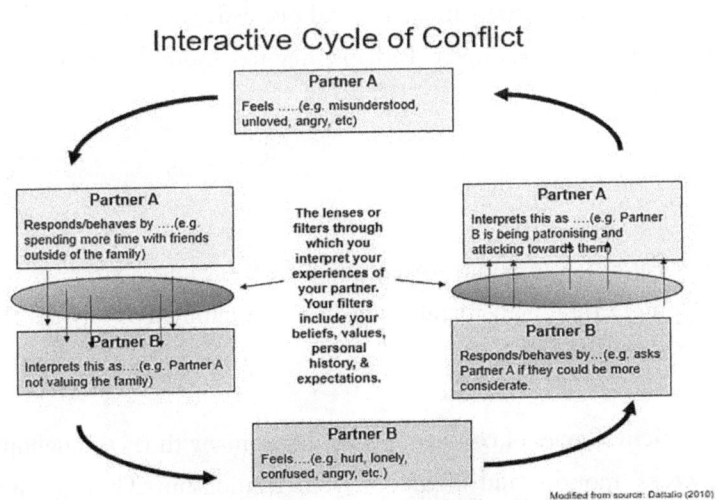

Diagram 1

Interactive Cycle of Conflict

Modified from source: Dattalio (2010)

- Partner A does or says something. In the example in Diagram 1 above, they are late home because they stayed out longer than expected chatting with friends.
- Through their experiential lenses/filters, Partner B interprets this negatively. Partner B has very strong family values and enjoys the time of the day when the family gets back together at the end of the day. Partner B sees Partner A's behaviour as not valuing the family.
- Partner B feels upset. Perhaps they feel hurt, confused, angry or let down.
- As the feelings manifest and intensify for Partner B, they respond by saying or doing something. Partner B asks Partner A if they could be more considerate of their family.
- Through their experiential lenses/filters, Partner A interprets Partner B's response/behaviour negatively. Partner A enjoys the time they spend with friends as it helps them to wind-down from

the drudgery of work before returning home. They regard Partner B's comments as patronising and dismissive of their needs.
- Partner A feels upset. Perhaps they feel misunderstood, unloved, or angry.

Then to complete the cycle:

- Partner A responds by repeating the behaviour. Partner A spends more time with friends outside of the family. Possibly debriefing about Partner B.

Interactive cycles of conflict operate many, many times throughout the day, weeks, months, and lifetime of your relationship. They are inevitable. Most of the time they are resolved with effective communication and understanding and go unnoticed. At other times, they can cycle around and gather in intensity. If left unchecked, they can lead to more serious conflicts and difficulties in your relationship.

During moments of time-out from an intense conflict, map out the cycle of interaction. Once this becomes clear, it is easier for partners to understand each other and discuss how the cycle can be interrupted before it gets worse.

In the example in Diagram 1, possible interventions could be:

- Partner A will organise other times to spend with their friends or will find a compromise with Partner B in an agreed time to be home.
- Partner B might better understand Partner A's need to unwind and not be too quick to interpret this time as devaluing the family.

- Partner B might rephrase their request to Partner A to include 'I' statements about how they feel and their desire for Partner A to come home sooner.
- Partner A might better understand how Partner B is feeling and see this as a need for support rather than a personal attack.

Note 6: *It is important to note when you are looking for ways to interrupt an interactive cycle of conflict that you don't overly focus on changing your feelings. Going for a walk and having time-out can certainly provide short-term relief by reducing your body tensions and de-escalating your feelings. However it is by challenging and changing your perceptions and behaviour that will affect a longer-term result.*

Just as negotiation skills require thoughtful practice, effective interpersonal communication requires both partners to be able to step away from the content of their conversation and from time to time do a preventative health check on their communication styles. Admittedly, there may be times when your partner simply does not want to hear what you have to say. Nevertheless, the effectiveness of your communication will always be measured on how well your partner understands what you are meaning to communicate.

If you get a sense that you and your partner are becoming increasingly out-of-sync with each other, schedule a time together to talk about your respective communication styles:

- Are you more verbally expressive and like to talk things out as you are thinking them through? or
- Do you tend to mull things over before you offer them up in conversation?

- Do you feel more comfortable talking thoughts and ideas rather than feelings and beliefs?
- Check-in with your partner from time-to-time and get some feedback about your communication.
  - Ask about how well your partner feels listened to and understood.
  - Ask your partner how well they feel that they know your thoughts, opinions, feelings and beliefs about things. Have some fun by testing it out by asking them to guess your views on a controversial or ethical topic.
  - If you're feeling brave, ask your partner what they think has been the most important issue ruminating around your mind lately. If they are correct, thank them for their appreciation of you. If otherwise, spend a little time bring them into the frame.
  - Finally, check whether there are any unresolved issues that need to be put-to-bed.

Note 7: *Before I leave the topic of communication there is one more piece of wisdom that I would like to add. If you start to experience some tension and difficulty in your conversations, whether they be verbal or written, check and ask yourself, "Who actually or symbolically am I conversing with here?" or "Who are they reminding me of?", or "Which version of this person is present in my mind?" It is possible that unconscious fears of non-present people, such as ex-partners, parents, work colleagues, bosses, etc, are bubbling way in your unconscious, or perhaps past events, such as moments of trauma, shame, or distress.*

CARDIAC ARRYTHMIA – CLUMSY COMMUNICATION AND CONFLICT

During mediation sessions significant breakthroughs in communication can result when separated clients are reminded to converse with the other parent of your children (who loves your children as much as you do} rather than my ex-partner with whom I associate hurt and pain in my life (and whom I would like to even the score).

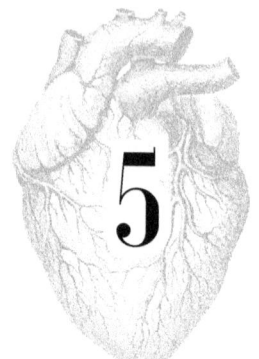

Congestive Cardiac Failure - Sharing Responsibilities

Heart failure refers to the heart's inability to pump blood efficiently. With heart failure, although the heart maintains some of its functionality for pumping blood around the body, it's poor condition results in blood returning to the heart faster than the heart can pump it out. Consequently, the blood flow to the heart becomes congested and other parts of the body are deprived of oxygen. A person with congestive cardiac failure may have shortness of breath, fatigue, swollen legs and rapid heartbeat.

CONGESTIVE CARDIAC FAILURE - SHARING RESPONSIBILITIES

The freedom to be yourself, to step out of your other social roles, and to be spontaneous with your intimate partner is one of the life-sustaining benefits of your relationship. How good is it to be able to speak your inner thoughts free from the fear of being judged as ignorant, naïve, or politically incorrect. To be able to don your daggiest, yet most comfortable clothes, to sing out of tune, to make corny jokes, and talk to the TV screen to warn your favourite character of impending danger. Although the list can go on indefinitely, like all life functions our intimate relationships require a degree of organisation, defined responsibilities, planning, and deliberate action.

> *Intimate relationships require a degree of organisation, defined responsibilities, planning and deliberate action*

Couples can have clearly defined and delineated tasks, like one partner assuming responsibility for cleaning the bathrooms and doing the laundry, while the other partner clears the gutters and maintains the lawns and garden. Other couples might share all their tasks, but even in the world of gender fluidity, they might take turns as who is going to do what and when.

When it comes to the pragmatic areas of intimate relationships it's important not to assume:

- not to assume that your partner will take-on responsibility for the tasks that may have been gender assigned from your parents.
- not to assume that your partner will place the same level of importance to a particular task as you do.
- not to assume your partner always enjoys the tasks they volunteer to do regularly.
- not to assume your partner no longer requires your expressions of gratitude.

- not to assume that your partner can mindread your thoughts and understand your feelings at every moment and on every issue.
- not to assume that, because your partner loves you, they will be available to give you 100% of their attention and empathy when you are most in need – that is, you are stressed and tired.

Like your heart, your intimate relationship is susceptible to inefficiencies. Things just don't function as smoothly as you would like, well, not all the time anyway. For example: bills don't get paid on time, clothes washing builds up, the grass grows high, take-away meals become more frequent, important appointments are missed, you forget important dates, and routines are lost. Like the blood flowing back to the heart for reoxygenation, so also are the number of tasks impinging on your relationship that demand time and attention. And when your various roles lose their efficiency, the tasks build up, they get congested, and they will threaten to smother the life out of your relationship.

Case History

Gregory and his wife were able to sort out most of the day-to-day tasks of co-habitation early on in their relationship. It seemed pretty much the same as when they first moved into shared accommodation with fellow students at university. They were able to establish a cooking and cleaning roster and had candid conversations about other areas of household management. Then came the birth of their first child. Apart from having to come to grips with the idea of now being parents, they were faced with new co-habiting tasks that they had neither previous experience nor sufficient preparation. On top of everything else they needed to do to maintain a happy household, they now had nappy (diaper) changes, feeding, nursing and rocking to sleep, pushing the pram, sterilising equipment, strapping the child in the car capsule, etc. Gregory assumed this was all 'women's work' and his partner could simply absorb this into her regular daily routine. Because his partner gave up full-time work to nurture their infant, Gregory also assumed that he could come home from work each day, collapse on the couch and have his wife wait on him. The reality check came quick, firm and fast.

The tasks and responsibilities that require our attention and negotiation in an intimate relationship are infinite and relentless. There may be times when you think that you are on top of them all, but these are few and far between. For the most part, there is a constant backlog of 'round tuits', that is, things you will get around to it one day. Effectively and efficiently managing the endless list of tasks and responsibilities as a couple is key to a healthy relationship.

When people are stressed and tired and feel overburdened with the mundane and demanding tasks of life it is very, very easy to slide into the comfortable 'woe is me' mindset. It's a pattern of thought, an internal script, that goes along the line of "how come I am the only one doing the heavy lifting around here?", or worse, "does he/she think I am here as their slave to serve them?" Whenever (not IF ever) you are tempted to get the grumbles about the size of your workload or your superior performance record compared to your partners, pull yourself up immediately, hopefully before you mouth-it-off to your partner. Factually you might even be correct, but relationally you are venturing into 'the devil's playground'. Instead, recognise that your workload, your stress, your frustrations and your tiredness are YOUR experience. You need to own your experience and make whatever changes you should make to yourself without expecting any changes from your partner. Yes, it is helpful to express your experience to your partner, but not in the words of blaming, accusations and demands. Apart from being counterproductive and disempowering, expecting your partner to take responsibility for your miserable moment will likely arouse their defensiveness and begin to drive a wedge of distance between you. This might only be momentary, and you take timeout to cool down and talk about it again later; or it could become a pattern of behaviour that leads to more and more resentment of each other and greater and greater distance.

So now we know what not to do, let's explore some of the more helpful task management strategies.

Firstly, do 'sweat the small stuff'. It's amazing just how much of an impact is made when the smallest, what people might consider the trivial, tasks are attended to. Examples that readily come to mind may include making the coffee, cleaning the dishes after dinner, replacing the roll of toilet paper or toothpaste, pumping up the bike tyres, vacuuming the carpet, dusting the cupboard, dealing with your dirty washing, and of course there is the proverbial toilet seat being placed up or down. This list is endless, but my point is profound. Paying diligent attention to the small tasks is the lubricating oil that maintains the smooth, day-to-day functioning of your interactive relationship.

Squabbles and grumbles about the small tasks, however, are the canary in the coal mine. They are the first indicators that things might be festering and in need of attention regarding the big-ticket items. And the biggest of them all is the time and energy spent in gainful employment verses the time and energy spent with childcare and household management. On the balance sheet we have dollars on one side and in-kind contributions on the other side.

Case History – A – Fictional but Typical

Frank comes home from work. It's mid-week and the weekend is far from sight. He is stressed and tired and envisions himself throwing off his work clothes, having a shower and collapsing on the couch with a cup of tea or cold beer. Instead, he gets greeted by his partner talking on the telephone to a friend, the kids are running riot, and the house is a mess. His emotional triggers become cocked and ready to fire. Then, there is no milk in the fridge to put in his cup of tea.

Case History – B - Fictional but Typical

Mary, Frank's wife, has been caring for three children throughout the day. Two of the kids were on school vacation and the third was an infant. It's been a long day catering for meals, changing diapers, dealing with sibling fights, claims of unfairness, and screams to get attention. Venturing out to the shops would be a nightmare and doing the housework is not her priority. She is hanging out for Frank to return home from work to give her a little respite from the torment of yelling and screaming kids. Then, her best friend calls to share some bad news just as Frank comes home. He ignores the kids and proceeds to make himself a cup of tea.

Note: in the case histories A & B above, this is not the time to have a conversation about who is doing the heavy lifting in this relationship. Both partners are stressed and tired and the risk of emotions escalating, particularly with the kids present, is way too high. This would be the time to remind yourself that you have no idea what has led to this moment in your partner's day, put everything else to the side, even the kids, and take a moment to chill-out together.

Eventually, hopefully sooner rather than later, partners will need to have the difficult conversations (note plural) about sharing the workload. When doing so it is important to recognise that these conversations are far less about the actual equity in the distribution of tasks and more about feelings of detachment, being unsupported, and a lack of appreciation. You would do well not to launch into these sorts of conversations by listing, negotiating and assigning all the things that need to be done to maintain the relationship – e.g. income generation, taxiing the kids, paying the bills, doing the laundry, maintaining the house and garden, organising parties and events, etc. And it would be far from helpful to do an appraisal of each other's work performance in their role as a partner.

The most helpful thing is to talk about your mutual desires and goals to support each other in ALL that needs to be done. To talk about the moments when you are most vulnerable to feelings of being unsupported. That is, when you are most likely to be feeling stressed, tired, overwhelmed, frustrated, confused, etc. To talk about how you can flag these moments with each other and what the things your partner could do that would be most helpful at these times.

Obviously, you will need to have conversations to determine the division of tasks in your relationship, whether they be by an ongoing or day-to-day agreement. Just be aware that there will be times when you assume that things would have been attended to by your partner only to find out otherwise. And there will be times when your partner requests that you

Just be aware that there will be times when you assume that things would have been attended to ..only to find out otherwise

attend to something when your 'cup is already full'. It's at these times you will appreciate the preliminary work you would have done understanding and communicating with each other.

Case History – C & D – Fictional

It was Sunday mid-afternoon and John, and his partner were sharing their foreseeable thoughts on the coming week. It was the busy season at John's worksite, and he felt under the pump to reach the ridiculous deadlines his boss had set. To make matters worse he had a meeting with his boss on Wednesday right in the middle of the day when he was hoping to focus on more critical parts of his project. He mentioned to his partner that if he came home late and dishevelled on Wednesday evening, he might need a little time to shake off the day before he gave his attention to the kids.

Cleo, John's wife, mentioned how she had planned to keep the kids occupied during the school vacation. She also mentioned the concern she had for her best friend whose father was at end-of-life. She said she wasn't sure when her friend's father might die, only that she wanted to support her friend when she needed her. Whenever John and Cleo were on an important telephone call they would signal to each other with their index finger to their lips.

As stated, the above case histories are fictitious and there can be untold variations of the theme. That being: how easy it is to reach flashpoint when the focus of your thoughts, your words, your actions is merely on the practical tasks – the things that need doing in your relationship. Pre-emptive conversations that involve foreseeable or potential moments of difficulty, fragility and/or vulnerability, and mitigating strategies for managing such moments is much more helpful than spending time divvying up the tasks and arguing/negotiating about who is going to do what, when and how.

> *Conversations that involve foreseeable or potential.... difficulty, fragility and/or vulnerability, and mitigating strategies....is much more helpful than ...divvying up the tasks...*

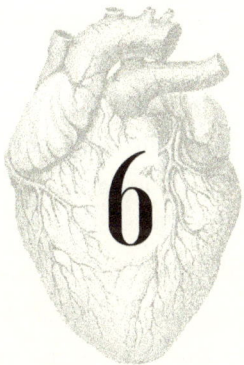

Cardiomyopathy – The build-up of tension

Cardiomyopathy is a disease of the heart muscle that affects its ability to pump blood around the body. Hypertrophic cardiomyopathy is when the heart muscle enlarges and thickens, making the chambers of the heart narrow and difficult for it to pump blood. Restrictive cardiomyopathy is when the heart chambers become stiff and rigid and cannot relax and fill with enough blood to pump. Cardiomyopathy can be genetically inherited and/or caused by chronic hypertension and other factors.

Hypertension is the technical term used when referring to high blood pressure. It is when the force exerted on the inside walls of your blood vessels is persistently above what is deemed to be healthy. The pressure in your blood vessels alternates with each heartbeat – in the moments when your heart is contracting, your blood pressure rises; between contractions, your blood pressure returns to its resting pressure.

It is typical of all intimate relationships to have moments of tension and conflict – it is to be expected. Despite what delusions we might have about ourselves and/or our partners, and how wonderful we might think we/they are, we are all different and from time to time we will not see eye-to-eye, and we may need to resort to using some of our empathy, negotiating and conflict resolution skills.

For some people, the anxiety aroused, even with the hint of potential conflict, leads them to avoid conversations with their partner about important issues and depriving themselves of opportunities to grow together. Over time a steady and pathological build-up of residual tensions will develop, which if left unchecked could stiffen and harden their relationship, progressing to the development of rigid patterns of conversations, behaviour and activities, and restricting the flow of love, joy and creativity. It becomes quite unhealthy if one or both partners live in a state of fearfulness or walking on eggshells' when they are with their partner. This may become the precursor to challenges with anxiety and depression, co-dependence and domestic violence.

> *By avoiding difficult conversations ....a steady and pathological build-up of residual tensions will develop which, if left unchecked could "stiffen and harden" their relationship*

The risk of developing cardiomyopathy due to high blood pressure can be reduced with a number of lifestyle changes a person can make to lower their blood pressure. These include regular exercise, healthy diet, reducing salt intake, limiting alcohol consumption, cutting back on caffeine, etc. Similarly, there are many everyday changes a couple can make to their communication to lower the tension in their relationship and allow them to address conflict in a healthy and constructive manner. However, also like the lifestyle habits associated with high blood pressure, communication habits develop over a lifetime and breaking those habits will require discipline and intentional practice.

> *Communication habits develop over a lifetime and breaking those habits will require discipline and intentional practice*

Note 8*: Practice makes (~~perfect~~) possible.*

When couples become aware of some of their unhelpful styles of communication and decide to change, structuring a conversation, particularly if there is a build-up of tension and/or addressing a conflict, can feel awkward, clumsy and contrived. This is to be expected. A most unhelpful response to your partner during these times is to ridicule them or doubt their intentions. If it feels like you are being manipulated it is quite possible that you are – not by your partner, but by the structure of the conversation which is challenging you to rethink your unhelpful communication style. Even couples who generally have healthy communication habits might resort to a structured conversation when an issue is contentious and emotionally loaded.

> *Couples who generally have healthy communication habits might also resort to a structured conversation when an issue is contentious*

For structured conversations you need to be aware of a few 'do's' and 'don'ts':

Do's

a) Do choose an appropriate, comfortable setting and allow yourselves ample time to have the conversation.

b) Do express ownership of your thoughts, beliefs and opinions, and feelings. This could be done by prefacing your statements with 'I' For example: "I think this is the item we should purchase because…"; "I feel a little upset by what you said about my mother…" ; "I believe the government in this country would do well if…"

c) Do actively listen to your partner's statements to identify the content (thoughts, beliefs, opinions) and any feelings they are 'owning' by paraphrasing them back as a reflection and indication that you have heard them. Keep reflecting until they indicate that you have heard them clearly and correctly.
d) Do ask inquisitive and relevant questions.
e) Do give each other equal airtime.

Dont's

a) Don't expect to change your partner's position. If they need to change or shift their position on an issue let them do this themselves.
b) Don't extend the conversation beyond the level of tension you can both cope with. If you need to call time-out do so in agreement that you will return to the conversation at a specified time.
c) Don't blame, accuse, ridicule, raise your voice, dominate the airtime, make threats, or give ultimatums.
d) Don't check or even look at your mobile device – hide it away or turn it off.

Note 9: For the sake of diplomacy, if your partner doesn't preface their statements with 'I', make a thoughtful adjustment in your mind as if they are expressing ownership over whatever they are saying.

Unhelpful communication habits can also include some embedded, and mostly unconscious, assumptions and distortions that can infiltrate your

|| *Unhelpful communication habits can also include some imbedded, and*

thinking, sabotage a conversation, even a structured conversation, and elevate the level of tension between partners. Some of the more identifiable culprits are:

- **Overgeneralisations** – often identified when a person uses absolute words like always and never such as: "You *never* listen to me"; or "I'm *always* asking you to…"

- **Magnification and minimisation** – unjustifiably attributing greater or lesser credence and importance to things/events/people that collude with a person's position on an issue. For example: "If I can get this job finished it will mean we will be comfortable for the rest of our lives (magnifying)"; or "You don't have to worry about all the time I spend with my work colleague, he/she is just a friend (minimising)."

- **Mental filtering** – neglecting to recall things pertinent to the issue. Often identified by a person focussing only on the negative events and omitting the positive. For example: "Ever since we started going out together we have been arguing"; or "Whenever you play with the kids you become bossy."

- **Catastrophising** – often identified by speaking about problems as being huge and with possible devastating consequences. For example: "I don't want to talk about it because it will be the end of our relationship"; or "I will lose my job if I don't get to work on time today."

- **Jumping to conclusions** – neglecting to consider all the options regarding a person's motives, rationales, possible outcomes and other missing information. There are different ways to interpret any given situation.

- **Personalising** – often identified when a person consistently blames themselves or blames their partner when things go wrong.

- **Black and white thinking** – often identified by a person taking a position of all or nothing, good or bad, right or wrong and neglecting to consider middle ground options or areas of ambiguity

- **Unrealistic expectations** – often identified when a person uses the words 'ought', 'should or 'must'.

Modified from source: https://iqdoodle.com/cognitive-distortions/

Like most habits in life, unhelpful styles of communication function unconsciously. The first step to ensuring these habits don't develop in your relationship, or if they need breaking, is to bring them into your conscious awareness. When you're together discussing difficult issues, be mindful of any feelings of tension to alert you to the possibility that one or more of these unconscious habits is trying to sabotage your conversation. Then together deal with it/them as you would a lifestyle habit that risked the health of your heart.

Case History

Jarrod prided himself on his DYI (Do It Yourself) abilities. He could turn his hand to most manual tasks with tradesman like skills. So, when it came to entering into an intimate relationship it was only reasonable for him to assume, (in all honesty, he probably didn't even think about it at all), that he could simply wing it, and if the relationship started to become unstuck, he would be able to fix it. Well, things did become unstuck and unfortunately for Jarrod the more difficult things became the more his ego hardened, and he refused to seek or accept any professional help. During a mediation session with Jarrod and Kymberly, his now former partner, to determine the co-parenting arrangements for the children and property settlement, Jarrod didn't miss his opportunity to demonstrate his self-learned interpersonal communication skills. To quote a few of his remarks: "It always has to be her way and it's going to end up in a mess"; "The system is stacked against men and she is going to get everything"; "She was like this all the time when we were together." He couldn't see that he didn't have the tools in his toolbox when it came to healthy and effective interpersonal communication. If he had recognised early in the relationship that he was not so competent in interpersonal communication, perhaps the relationship could have survived and his need for mediation could have been avoided.

Distorted communication habits can develop equally in both men and women and be present in one or both partners in an intimate relationship. They don't just spring up overnight. On reflection some people can recognise the distorted communication styles from the get-go. Indeed, they develop in childhood, in one's family of origin. In the early stages of a relationship, they usually go unnoticed and may even be complimentary. For example, one partner may comment, "I love the way you are always able to fix things"; or "I like to be decisive and get on with the job" or "Hey, don't worry about the ... it will sort itself out." They may not seem problematic in the context of being a positive, affirming statement, but they are the same distorted communication styles that slowly and insidiously creep into other less affirming conversations, including your times of conflict.

It is imperative that a couple learn to recognise their distorted communication styles and be confident and feel safe to check each other when they automatically use an unhelpful expression. It takes time and deliberate effort to break old habits and learn new ways to express yourself. To ignore the old habits or take a DYI approach to your communication runs the risk of your heart walls gradually hardening.

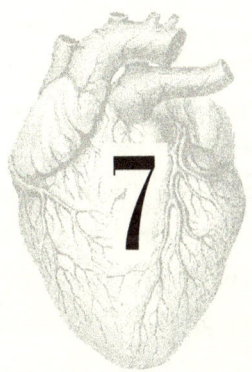

Coronary heart disease – Loss of Passion

Atherosclerosis: is when the main arteries that supply your heart muscle with oxygen-rich blood, your coronary arteries become narrowed by a gradual build-up of fatty material within their walls. A heart attack occurs when a coronary artery becomes completely blocked and there is a sudden deprivation of blood circulating to the heart muscle causing necrosis (death) to a part of the heart.

Arteriosclerosis: is the stiffening or hardening of the artery walls by a build-up of fibrous tissue and calcification. Your blood vessels become less responsive and resilient to variations in the blood pumping around your heart and the rest of your body.

Anticipating your partner's feelings, thoughts and behaviours with a reasonable degree of consistency contributes to the level of trust we have in our partners and enables us to be confident and relaxed with them. We relate to our partners without having to continually monitor our words and actions and second guess how our partners will respond.

The downside to becoming overly comfortable with the routines in our lives and the predictability of our partners is the risk of becoming lazy in our relationship, taking our partners for granted, and overlooking their growth as individuals. Like the arteries that supply the oxygen-rich blood to our heart, the activities that supply life-giving love to our relationships become hard and clogged up with distractions such as our work, paying the bills, other family members, health issues, and other outside interests. We also run the risk of becoming less responsive to the feelings of our partners and equally, we risk becoming insensitive to the loving gestures they make towards us.

> *Becoming overly comfortable with the routines in our lives and the predictability of our partners is the risk of becoming lazy in our relationship*

A couple who have been together for a good length of time might become quite abrupt in their communication with each other. From a visitor's point of view their communication may appear abusive and yet the couple seem oblivious to it, and don't appear to have any hard feelings as a result of the words spoken to them by their partners (I find these moments very awkward). It's as if the couple have become so accustomed to each other that they take short-cuts in

> *A couple may become so accustomed to each other that they take short-cuts in their expressive communication and neglect to cushion their conversations with respectful language*

their expressive communication and neglect to cushion their conversation with respectful language.

Coronary heart disease insidiously creeps up on its unsuspecting target until they start to feel the first pain of angina. Angina is a chest pain symptom of coronary artery disease. It is a tightness, pain, or discomfort in the chest that occurs when an area of the heart muscle receives less blood oxygen than usual. Likewise, the first symptom of a disease in your relationship could be your physical and/or mental health, your lack of interest in sex, frequent and unresolved arguments, and looking outside of your relationship for sources of love and joy.

Understanding the circulatory nature of love is a key to sustaining a healthy flow within your relationship as well as to others around you. It goes like this: you need to receive love to be able to give love, then you need to give love to receive love. It sounds paradoxical to think you need to give away what little you may have to receive more, but that is the circulatory nature of love. You will notice it has a sort of multiplying effect when it returns to you. This also applies to things like nature, art, music, literature, and spiritual practice. Give back to nature by attending to your garden or picking up a piece of litter in the park, immerse yourself in a piece of art, music or literature, and schedule a time of devotion for your spiritual practice. The more love you give, the more you will be able to receive.

Re-opening the love flow to your relationship can have a powerful rejuvenating impact on the health of your relationship. Gary Chapman has written extensively on five love languages that can be deliberately adopted to increase the supply of love-rich vitality to your relationship:

> Quality Time: this artery is likely to be the one most clogged, especially if you have a young family, a demanding career, and a smart device welded to your body like an additional appendage. It is so, so easy to give priority to everything other than spending

quality time with your partner. That is, time where being together with your partner is your primary purpose. It might be as simple as sitting beside each other whilst you are both reading; shopping, cooking or doing the dishes together, spending time in the garden, playing scrabble, chatting over a cup of coffee, etc, etc. Or it might be something more extravagant like taking a travelling holiday, or trip on a cruise ship. The list is endless but the most important thing to be mindful of is not to make the activity/event the primary purpose for your being together. Sure, you might be focused on, say, the movie you are watching together at the cinema, or the colour of the wall you are painting together. However, what quality time means is that you would choose rather to not do the activity if your partner were not doing it with you.

> *What quality time means is that you would choose to rather not do the activity if your partner were not doing it with you*

Note 10: *Put your smart phone away. I equate this to someone having a stent inserted into a coronary artery to increase the blood flow to the heart and then proceeding to pig-out on cream cakes.*

Also, if you're brave enough to add a little romantic touch to your quality time together, try voicing it to your partner. Regardless of what you are doing, tell them how much you enjoy simply spending time with them. [5]

<u>Words of Affirmation:</u> **words of affirmation are complimentary to your partner. They serve to build up your partner and show honour to them.**

---

[5] Woo Hooo! Then brace yourself for a rush of blood.

Whether spoken in private or in the presence of others they can enrich the bond of connection between you both.

Increasing the flow of love through this artery is particularly helpful for a couple who have become so familiar with each other in their daily lives that they no longer SEE their partner as they did when they first fell in love. Worse still, when their language no longer affords the same level of respect to their partner that they would otherwise show to another person, even a stranger.

Expressions of gratitude (e.g. please, thank you, that's great, perfect, etc) are probably one of the most basic forms of words of affirmation. The scarcity or absence of expression of gratitude between partners is a sure symptom of hardening of this artery.

At worst, this artery is most damaged when verbal abuse is present in the relationship. This could include making negative, mean or insulting comments, gaslighting, making threats, using vulgar language towards the partner, or yelling at them. Such behaviours hurt and belittle your partner and are best treated immediately as an autoimmune disease (see chapter 13). That is, it needs to stop and stop now.

Increasing the flow of love to your relationship through words of affirmation you will need to be:

a) Deliberate – just as it may have taken a long time to have fallen into a habit of neglecting to give words of affirmation to your partner, shaking the habit will take you some time. Indeed, throughout the life of your relationship you may have to be forever vigilant not to fall back into the habit. You can't just tell yourself that this is a good idea and you will try to take it on board. You will need to plan for and discipline yourself to offer daily compliments.

b) Genuine – you and your partner might find it a little artificial at first as you practice giving your words of affirmation, but this should not mean they are any less genuine. Your partner has an infinite number of positive qualities – have fun discovering or rediscovering them. Also, keep in mind that patronising or sarcastic compliments will back-fire badly and will most likely lead to further hardening of this artery.

c) Simple – expressions of gratitude are very simple and although it may seem like they might lose their impact over time, make a mental note to tell yourself that they never go un-noticed. Compliments can also be simple, such as "You did well with that" or "I like the way you did that." Long-winded affirmations can be saved for weddings and funerals.

<u>Acts of Service:</u> Most relationships have some level of mutual sharing of responsibilities for the tasks and chores of daily living. Without meaning to minimise the importance of each partner fulfilling their share of tedious responsibilities, taking deliberate action to increase the flow of love to your relationship through Acts of Service will involve sacrificing some of your time and making an effort to do something with the primary purpose of increasing your partner's happiness.

> *Acts of Service will involve sacrificing some of your time and making an effort to do something with the primary purpose of increasing your partner's happiness*

An effective Act of Service is thoughtful of your partner's well-being and is done with alacrity. That is, you need also to have a positive attitude as you perform this activity for your partner. Moaning and grumbling as you engage in the activity will most certainly take any shine off your endeavours to increase your flow of love through this artery.

An Act of Service for your partner is less effective if it is done as a payback for something they may have done for you – a sort of balancing the score card. It most certainly should not be done with the expectation that your partner now owes you one.

Like words of affirmation, increasing the flow of love to your relationship through Acts of Service you will need to be:

a) Deliberate – there is no doubt that many Acts of Service that demonstrate your love and appreciation to your partner can be spontaneous. You might notice them struggling with a task and so you break away from whatever you are focused on at the time to lend your partner a hand. Relying on the spontaneity, however, has the risk of you not noticing anything and before long, despite your good intentions, nothing has changed. Make a short-list of things you can begin to do to make life easier for your partner and start with those.

b) Genuine – Acts of Service are primarily about your partner's happiness and need to be meaningful to them. Even though you may experience your own benefits because of a particular act of service, front and centre of your motivation is the happiness and wellbeing of your partner. For example, if your partner habitually attends to making the bed each morning, although you will benefit from having your bed made up, your goal for making the bed as an Act of Service is to bring happiness to your partner. Also, should you perform an Act of Service that is more meaningful to you than to your partner, you might experience a sense of frustration when the response from your partner is less impressive than what you expected.

c) Simple – Acts of Service that have the most immediate impact are usually the small things. Sure, it can be wonderful when you complete a large, complex and longer-term project for your partner, but these are few and far between. Try surprising your partner with frequent little actions that positively disrupt your partner's expectations.

<u>Gifts</u>: In my childhood I always equated the giving and receiving of gifts with birthdays and Christmas. I guess I could probably include Easter as well with the giving and receiving of chocolate Easter Eggs. Things didn't change all that much in adulthood, only that a few extra occasions came into the annual calendar, such as my wedding anniversary, Mother's Day and Father's Day. Being born into a culture of giving and receiving gifts at specific times of the year, I didn't come to fully appreciate the intended, deeper meaning of gift giving until later in life. That is, as a communication of love. On these occasions, the gift is a tangible representation of the intangible love that connects the giver and the receiver.

As with all communication, both the giver and the receiver have a role in the effectiveness of the communication process. The giver needs to be most mindful of their partner in the selection of the gift. They need to consider a gift that would bring joy to their partner. As with Acts of Service, gift giving also requires some form of sacrifice. This may include the cost of the item, spending

> *The level of thoughtfulness and sacrifice made by the giver speaks far louder than the monetary value of the gift*

time searching and shopping for the gift, the time to build or make the gift, and wrapping the gift. The more sacrifice of yourself in presenting the gift the clearer the message of love being expressed. It is important to remember that the material value of the gift is of very little significance in and of itself. This doesn't mean you have license to be a cheapskate. What it means is that the level of thoughtfulness and sacrifice made by the giver speaks far louder than the monetary value of the gift.

The receiver of the gift also has an important part to play. They need to receive the gift as a message of love, not merely as a pragmatic solution being offered to resolve an area of need, nor as a novel addition to their otherwise overcrowded collection of stuff. The gift itself is only a medium, a carriage for conveying the message of love. When I receive a gift that has been wrapped, I like to take the time to ponder on the effort that has been taken by the giver to wrap the gift. This offers me time before I get carried away with enjoying the gift itself to be mindful of the message of love they are expressing.

> *Receive a gift as a message of love, not merely as a pragmatic solution being offered to resolve an area of need*

Gifts can also be given in response to your partner's love language. For example, a gift is given as a demonstration of appreciation for a loving Act of Service they provided to you. It would be a mistake to understand this type of gift giving as pay-back to even up the love balance sheet. To regard it this way would be to denigrate your love relationship to a transactional one; a quasi-business arrangement where your gift could just as easily be converted into a cash payment. A gift given to your partner as a show of gratitude says to your partner that you acknowledge and have received their offer of love to you.

A gift is a wonderful way to clear up an artery to the heart of your relationship. The flow will be most strong when a gift is given, received and recognised as a communication of love between you and your partner.

<u>Physical Touch</u>: Physical touch is possibly the most intimate of the love languages and penetrates deep into the heart of your relationship. If this artery is significantly restricted or blocked, it is advisable to progress slowly, gently and respectfully as you endeavour to increase the flow of love to your relationship through physical touch.

For most of us, the safest area of touch would be the outside section of your forearm between your wrist and elbow. In the early stages of unblocking this artery, avoid stroking or caressing the arm. Simply place your hand on their arm when you want to communicate your love. It might be when you are watching a movie together, when you are sharing an intensely emotional experience with your partner, or when you're listening to your partner as they share something important and concerning to them. A touch of your hand on your partner's forearm to communicate your love is a good place to start, especially if this artery has been blocked for a length of time, or, because of your partner's history they associate physical touch with punishment or oppression.

The intimacy of physical touch is deepened with hugs, holding hands, shoulder rubs and foot massages. As with the other love languages, it might take you some time before you become almost unconscious with these forms of touch. Until then, you will need to make a deliberate effort. Talk to your partner and/or try out a few different touches. If your partner has long hair, try brushing their hair while you are watching a movie together, or try holding hands when you go for a walk. If these things haven't been a feature of your relationship for a long time or are new for you, both you and your partner might feel a little awkward and your actions may be a little uncoordinated at first. That's OK. Laugh together about it.

Physical touch can also be part of your daily rituals and still communicate a clear and meaningful message of love. The best example of this would be the brief kiss when you part for an extended period, and when you later reunite. Although the gesture may be ritualistic, it can nevertheless communicate the flow of love between you and your partner. There is an important proviso, however, when giving the kiss you still need to be mindful of your love for your partner. Kissing your partner farewell, while your mind is already preparing for your meeting, or trying to remember the best route to the airport, or whatever, is not likely to engender much intimacy.

The deepest form of physical touch is sexual intimacy and can play an important part in bonding between a couple. It's a paradoxical time when you and your partner are at your most vulnerable, yet also a time when you can feel incredibly safe, secure and accepted. Sexual intimacy is not necessarily sexual intercourse and visa-versa, sexual intercourse does not always involve sexual intimacy. Sexual intimacy is when the physical touch between you and your partner is all encompassing, sacred and spiritual.

> [Sexual intimacy is a] time when you and your partner are at your most vulnerable, yet also a time when you can feel incredibly safe, secure and accepted

Concerns about sexual intimacy are likely to surface many times for a couple. It could relate to one partner either not willing to engage in sexual intercourse, not satisfied or comfortable with the intercourse, or has lost interest in sex. Issues about sex can be both a cause of difficulties in an intimate relationship as well as a symptom of difficulties.

The sexual appetite for a couple or for one partner can wax and wane for many reasons and the issues involved can be complex and challenging to unravel. These include:

- Biochemical changes and fluctuations in the body, medications, physical exhaustion, stress, and depression.
- One or both partners no longer finding their partner sexually attractive.
- Concerns about performance, a lack of experience or knowledge.
- Feelings of guilt or shame, or a past sexual trauma or abuse.
- A couple have fallen out of the habit of having sex, perhaps following the birth of a child.
- One partner may be involved with someone else.

Although some people may find speaking openly about sexual matters highly uncomfortable, particularly in the present of a third person, seeking the support of a relationship counsellor/therapist is essential. Merely because one or both partners have lost interest in sex does not equate to a loss of love or hope in the relationship. As people age and as the relationship matures, the value of companionship intensifies and may surpass the desire for sex.

For younger couples it can be quite liberating to know you can have a healthy intimate relationship without sex. Even to the contrary: a young couple who have a very strong sexual attraction may choose to abstain from sex prior to marriage as a powerful demonstration of their love to each other.

> *It can be quite liberating to have a healthy intimate relationship without sex*

Rejuvenating your relationship by reopening your arteries of love is not a first-aid treatment. Nor is it an *ad lib* medication that you take from time to time when you feel the symptoms coming on. Re-establishing a strong flow of love throughout your relationship requires ongoing vigilance and application of your love languages.

> *Your relationship requires ongoing vigilance and application of your love languages*

Case History

Steve had a long history of perpetrating abusive behaviours on his intimate partner. When I first met him, he and his partner, Irene, were living apart. When I spoke with Irene she stated that she still loved him, but she would no longer tolerate his mean, belittling and deeply hurtful outbursts. Steve on the other hand said that he had experienced spiritual enlightenment and was now a different man. He wanted to move back to living together. He found it difficult to understand why his claim to being born again as a Christian and his verbal expressions of love were falling on deaf ears with his partner. With guidance and encouragement, he came to understand that the healing required to the damaged arteries of the heart required much more than words and good intentions. He had to learn how to demonstrate his love in a language that he hoped his partner would receive - for her it was words of affirmation. He had to practice formulating genuine affirmations and articulating them sensitively. He also had to accept that this would take time and that there was no guarantee or expectation as to how she would respond.

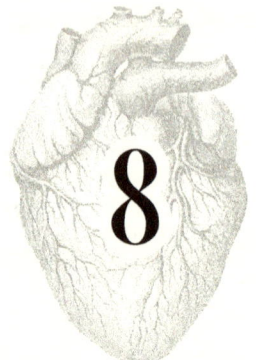

8

Hole in the Heart – The missing pieces

Holes in the heart occur in the dividing wall (septum) between the right and left chambers of the heart. A hole in the heart is a genetic defect.

If the hole is small, it may have minimal effect on heart function and many small holes close on their own. Medium or larger holes can result in a large amount of blood leaking from the heart's left side back to the right side and may need surgical repair early in life to prevent complications. Surgical repair requires a mesh patch or plug to cover the hole.

When most of us flow through the stream of life and begin to enter the pools and eddies of a long-term intimate relationship, we seldom ever stop to wonder if we are sufficiently equipped and prepared to traverse the journey ahead. Most, if not all, of our preparation for a long-term relationship comes from our genetic inheritance, our early childhood attachments, and the role models of our parents and other significant adults.

Despite how wonderful we might think of our genetic dispositions and/or the nurturing we received from our parents, no-one is ultimately coordinating our lives to ensure we are fully prepared for the momentous challenges we face when it comes to our own intimate relationships in adulthood. Consequently, as we venture into these relationships we can be blindsided by the complexity of relationship dynamics. We can place unrealistic expectations on ourselves and our partners, and/or we can realise that we have a bit of work to do to acquire the missing pieces that will patch up and plug the holes in our preparation.

> *No-one is ultimately coordinating our lives to ensure we are fully prepared for the momentous challenges we face when it comes to our intimate relationships*

There is so much that could be said about our genetic make-up and what we inherit from those who have gone before us. As well as our physical features such as the length and shape of our nose, hair colour, skin type, body morphology and the like, which are genetically inherited from our biological parents, research into how the life experiences of previous generations also affect our inherited epigenome is fascinating[6]. In laymen's terms, although the genome (complex combination of genes) we inherited from our parents is fixed and not altered by our life influences, our epigenome, which is affected by our life experiences is

---

[6] https://www.nature.com/articles/s41594-019-0239-5

also passed from generation to generation. Our epigenome serves to regulate which specific DNA sequences are expressed and those which remain dormant. In short, some of the contributions you make to your relationships are influenced by the dispositions you inherited from previous generations. That is, along with your genetic make-up some of the significant traumatic life events that were experienced by your grandparents and great grandparents may be indirectly affecting what you carry with you into your own adult relationships[7].

The way we approach our intimate relationships is also subconsciously learned by observing the antics of our parents or other significant adults as they have muddled their way through their own relationship journey. Our parents, other significant adults, and, for some people, celebrity idols, are significant influences on our core beliefs and values, and how we play out the roles in our intimate relationships.

Whether we choose to adopt the beliefs, values and gender roles of our parents or actively reject them, they are having an influence. For some people, the role models from their childhood may have been highly functional, articulating and personifying helpful beliefs and values, and clearly demonstrating how to do healthy relationships. For others, there may have been significant short-comings in the way their role models demonstrated relationships – very little love languages spoken, disrespect, intimate partner violence, etc – leaving serious holes in their preparation. Realistically, for most of us, if not all, the role models we grew up with demonstrated a combination of both helpful and unhelpful interpersonal behaviours, to a greater or lesser degree.

On a deeper more emotional level, we also become accustomed to the intimacy we experienced in our relationship with our parents when we were children and unconsciously search out this emotional familiarity when we

---

[7] This is relevant for further understanding of intergenerational trauma

enter our adult-to-adult intimate relationships. Attachment theory maintains that a strong emotional and physical attachment to at least one primary caregiver is critical to personal development. If our infant attachment was experienced as secure and nurturing, we adapt well during our childhood development and are better equipped to enter and sustain healthy relationships in adulthood. Alternatively, if our infant attachment was experienced with preoccupation, dismissiveness, anxiety, fear and avoidance from our primary caregiver, we are highly likely to enter adult relationships with significant emotional/psychological missing pieces.

> *Some dispositions may strengthen your relationships while others may leave a hole*

Whether genome, epigenome, infant attachment, or learning behaviours, some of the dispositions we carry with us may strengthen our capacity for intimate relationships, while others leave a hole.

It is common for couples to look to their respective partners to patch or plug the holes in their intimate adult relationships. Some people are initially drawn to the neediness of their partner as it gives them a sense of worth and personal validation. Others are drawn to the unspoken promise from their partner that they will help them patch and plug their holes. Yet for others, it's a mutual patching and plugging of each other's holes. As with holes in the heart, if they are small, they usually heal of their own accord and/or are inconsequential. However, if the holes are large, relying on your partner to cover the hole can lead to an unhealthy relationship, including control issues, anger, and resentment, withdrawal, and other intruders such as anxiety and depression, medical issues, addictions and over commitment to outside interests such as work, career, sport and/or hobbies.

Patching or plugging the personal deficits that you bring with you into your relationship is essentially your own responsibility. By the same token, helping your partner to deal with their own missing pieces also adds to the health of your relationship. It's not your responsibility to patch or plug your partner's holes, nor visa-versa, but it's important that you mutually acknowledge and understand each other's missing pieces and commit to supporting your partner as they grapple with the legacy issues that they inherited.

> *It's not your responsibility to patch or plug your partner's holes*

Identifying what's missing in yours or your partner's capacity to contribute to the health of your relationship can be narrowed down to four main areas:

- Skills – negotiation, communication, resourcefulness
- Adeptness in Love Languages – quality time, words of affirmation, acts of service, giving and receiving gifts, physical.
- Core beliefs
- Emotional Assurances – overcoming fear

Table 1 on the following page lists some of the identifiable core beliefs and fears, compensation attempts, and the sense of what is possibly missing in a person's emotional development:

TABLE 1

Core Belief or Fear	Unhelpful Attempt to Compensate	Sense of What is Possibly Missing
Abandonment	Possessiveness	Self-assurance and confidence
Mistrust and abuse	Suspicion	Safety and trust
Vulnerability	Defensive	Security
Social exclusion	Compliancy	Belonging
Not being good enough	Perfectionism	Being OK
Failure	Driven	Success
Subjugation	Aggressive	Empowerment
Dependency	Independent	Individuality
Disrespect	Entitlement	Self-Respect

With love and understanding an ongoing commitment from you and your partner to pursue a healthy relationship, you may choose to persevere to see if the holes in the heart of your relationship will heal of their own accord; you may intentionally work to acquire the missing pieces; you may elect to develop management strategies for living with each other's legacy issues, and/or you may want to consult a professional counsellor or therapist. Whatever you decide, the most important thing is not to expect that you and/or your partner to be perfect, nor to blame yourself or your partner when either of you are from time to time struggling.

> *Don't expect that you and/or your partner to be perfect*

Case History

After a few years of marriage Ken and his partner, Pauline, were experiencing some difficulties. Ken commented that "nothing was ever good enough" for Pauline. For her, she believed that he was a narcissist. They were initially attracted to each other because, well, she liked his self-confidence; he liked her pursuit of excellence. It all seemed like the perfect match at the time, but now they frankly despised each other's dispositions. Individual therapy helped each partner to gain insight into their own disposition and how it influenced and affected the other partner.

Ken carried a deep and unconscious fear that all others, including intimate partners, were not to be trusted. He approached life with the core belief that when he needed something important, he could only rely on himself and his own competencies. Pauline held a fear that she was never good enough. She approached life with a core belief that she (and her intimate partner) needed to be perfect in all things. As they later disclosed their personal insights into themselves in couples therapy, they could reflect on how these dispositions influenced their perceptions of the other, and how they could work at reinterpreting their partner's motives and consequently, feeling and responding differently.

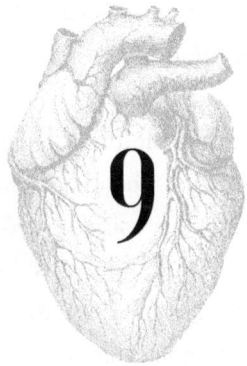

Cardiac Embolus – Maintaining boundaries

An embolism is when an embolus - a blood clot, fat globule, bubble of gas, or foreign material, which usually originates outside of the heart - moves through the blood stream, lodging itself inside one or more of the blood vessels in the heart, to obstruct or block the flow of blood through the heart, or to the muscle of the heart itself.

Often when people are reported to have had a sudden massive heart attack it is due to an embolism. In some cases, the warning signs can include pain or swelling in the leg, clammy skin, fever, light-headedness or dizziness - rapid or irregular heartbeat may not be immediately noticeable and/or come on very suddenly. In other cases, the warning signs have been present for some time and have gradually and insidiously intensified.

Setting the boundaries for an intimate relationship helps to protect the identity of the relationship and provides the infrastructure for developing and maintaining mutual trust, respect and safety for the growth of the individual partners, and for the relationship. When an outside influence, 'embolus', breaches a boundary and intrudes into your relationship, all the everyday issues that come as part-and-parcel of being in an intimate relationship are magnified and intensified.

An outside influence that has breached the boundary of an intimate relationship is not necessarily unlovable, bad or intrinsically evil. It has simply become problematic to the health of your relationship and if it persists could severely inhibit the development of your relationship or at worst damage and destroy it. By the same token, some outside influences may be considered pathological no matter what the context. For example addictions, medical conditions, and infidelity, and, although these are often more easily identified, their impact is equally, if not more difficult to manage.

Outside influences enter the relationship through one or both partners. There may be more than one outside influence having an unhelpful impact on your relationship and different partners may be responsible for facilitating the different influences.

Some of the more common outside influences that wreak havoc on a relationship are:

- Work/Career/Hobby
- Family and friends
- Chronic health issues
- Addictions, obsessions or fetishes
- Ghosts from the past
- A concurrent intimate relationship

This list is not meant to be exhaustive and there may be other outside influences that have the effect of there being a third person in a couple's relationship. For some people, it is the unhelpful intruder which may have been the very thing that attracted them to their partner in the first instance. For example, in your early dating period you may have admired and been attracted to your partner's sporting or business acumen. Today, it feels like you are competing against these very same things that steal away some of your partner's time and attention.

> *The unhelpful intruder which may have been the very thing that attracted you to your partner in the first instance*

Dealing with and managing an intrusive outside influence in your relationship requires a tremendous amount of empathy for the partner who is most engaged with the influence, and, if the outside influence happens to be a person, empathy for them as well.

A crucial step to dislodging the outside influence and its impact on your relationship is first to recognise and accept that the influence is highly important to the partner with whom it is attached. Similarly, acknowledging its effect on the other partner is also essential. Although it may be difficult for each partner to understand the strength of the attachment and impact, and it may seem highly irrational, when both partners are able to acknowledge the importance and impact of the outside influence on each other, without attempting to invalidate it, it reinforces the alliance between you and your partner. It also reduces the risk of both partners having an automatic defensive reaction when attempts are made to have an open discussion on how best the outside influence should be managed.

> *Recognise and accept that the influence is highly important to the partner with whom it is attached*

Equally important for addressing an outside influence is for both partners to separate outside influences from the partner to whom they are attached. Whether it is a medical condition, emotional baggage from the past, a mother-in-law or whatever, the outside influence is distinct from you, your partner, and the relationship. It may be a case of "love me, love my dog" but even in this cliché the person is deemed separate from the dog. Henceforth, when you and your partner are discussing the outside influence refrain from using individualised personal pronouns such as "your" illness, "my" career, "your" children" etc.

Where appropriate, replace personal pronouns with the word "the" to help separate the outside influence from you, your partner and your relationship. For example, "Let's talk about…:

…. the job"
…. the alcohol"
…. the back pain"
…. the depression
…. the football"
…. the children"

The next step: in an atmosphere of openness and trust clarify the effect the outside influence is having on your relationship. If you're able, discuss any benefits from having the outside influence as part of your life as well as the negative impact it is having on the relationship.

> **Note 11**: *Rather than the focus being on either you or your partner as individuals, it is helpful to keep returning the conversation back to the impact on your relationship.*

For example:

"I know the new job is important and requires a great deal of your time. It's been over 12 months now, and I am feeling a little isolated and alone here at home. I am concerned that we are becoming strangers in our relationship."

OR

"I know that watching the football on television helps you to unwind. There seems to be a game on every other evening, and I find it difficult to talk with you about things that have come up in my day. I wonder how we can manage the football, so we can spend a little more time together."

OR

"I know it is important for you to talk about the difficulties you had with 'Jane' (the ex-partner). You did well to come out of that relationship as strong as you have. The amount of airtime we give to talking about this person is robbing us from our own quality time together. What can we do to help reclaim our quality time and develop a strong relationship together?"

Work/Career/Hobby

Intimate relationships are not established, developed or sustained without sacrifice. The most visible sacrifice is the sacrifice of time. In the infancy of your relationship, you may have found it easier to give priority to your new relationship over things like your work, your sporting interests, music, art and other hobbies. Then as your relationship gradually develops you feel a 'calling' to return some of your attention to your outside interests. Indeed, this will be necessary, natural and

Each hour you accord to your outside interest is one less hour you have available to devote to your relationship

healthy. But there is only so much of your time to divvy up, and each hour you accord to your outside interests is one less hour you have available to devote to your relationship.

Finding the right balance between the time you assign your outside interests and the time you devote to your intimate relationship requires daily, weekly, and long-term joint management with you and your partner. Neglecting to discuss and agree to your respective daily schedules, your weekly commitments and your longer-term aspirations invite the risk for your outside interests to become outside intruders.

Each day requires you and your partner to have a brief mention of your respective demands, activities, and people you might meet during the day, as well as what time(s) you plan to reunite (in-person, telephone, video call, message, email, etc) during and/or at the end of the day. Unless there is a specific need, refrain from going into the detail – share enough of your day's schedule to ensure you and your partner understand and feel generally assured with your respective commitments.

Similarly, sharing each other's forthcoming weekly or monthly schedules can prevent any surprise commitments and time-clashes to lodge themselves into your relationship. All relationships function with a greater or lesser degree of routine and predictability, and it is easy for couples to assume that their respective partners are aware of their time commitments, and/or they simply overlook the need to inform them. If a pattern of neglect or forgetfulness to discuss each other's weekly or monthly commitments embeds itself into your relationship, there is a high risk that your outside commitments and time-clashes will become time-thieves.

You and your partner need to feel safe to pull back the curtain and discuss with each other your respective dreams and long-term vision

Most importantly, you and your partner need to feel safe to pull back the curtain and discuss with each other your respective dreams and long-term vision. For a couple this could involve a discussion about having children, career aspirations, where you would like to live, and what sort of lifestyle you would like to achieve. It may involve a discussion about your contributions to community, and your legacy. There is no doubt that we all change our vision and expectations for the future as we mature, and we will adjust our plans to align with our unfolding circumstances. Progressively, sharing your long-term hopes and dreams can help you to understand and accommodate each other's short and medium-term desires, and to negotiate around the things that compete for your limited time.

Family and Friends

An intimate relationship is generally accepted by each partner as an exclusive relationship. No other person is privileged to enjoy the same level of intimacy as that between the couple. It's a sacred area where the things shared are intensely private, where your emotional safety is at its most vulnerable, where the trust you offer and the loyalty you receive is at its highest.

When entering an intimate relationship, people are also transitioning from other relationships that have involved a similar level of closeness. For example:

- a parent or sibling of one or both partners
- a long-standing best friend, business partner or work colleague
- the partner and/or children from your previous intimate relationship

At times a healthy transition from your previous close relationships can become stalled and, despite how much you love these people, they run the risk of becoming unhelpful outside influences to your emerging intimate relationship.

I mentioned above that, where the outside influence happens to be a person, it is also helpful to empathise with that person to try to understand what might be inhibiting them from letting go and allowing you or your partner to transition into your new intimate relationship. That is, what is it that is so important to them that your relationship has become a source of need or comfort? For example, a parent, sibling or best friend of a partner may be fearful of losing and/or grieving the loss of their own attachment with you; it could be that they are anxious about their own future; jealous of your new envisioned destiny, and/or concerned about a practical need.

Parents also have their own history of relationships, both good and bad, and are notorious for projecting their issues, advice, opinions and solutions on to their children. Some of their involvement in your relationship may be helpful but at other times it can be distorted and unhelpful. For example, a parent who lived through domestic violence will want to ensure their child is safe and, in their hypervigilance, may catastrophise when they hear about natural incidents of conflict in their child's relationship.

Although the loving family member or friend will most likely be attached to one partner rather than to the couple, it is still important to work together as a couple to find a solution to their unhelpful outside influence. Spend time together: to empathise with the feelings of the outside person and to clarify how their involvement in your life is hindering your relationship. Also to agree to the changes that are required for the health

> *It is still important to work together as a couple to find a solution to their unhelpful outside influence*

of your relationship, and, if necessary, to formulate how this will be sensitively and respectfully communicated to the family member or friend.

For example:

> "Jane, you and I have been very close for most of our lives. Your relationship with me is very precious to both of us. Over the past year I have been leaning on you to find solutions to some of my difficult issues. To help me and my (new) partner grow together as a couple, my partner and I will need to spend more time alone together working through our tough issues."

OR

> "Mum, it is wonderful how you and I have such a close relationship. Letting go and putting trust in my partner must be quite challenging. Since my partner and I have been together we have been struggling to find time together for intimacy. Instead of visiting so frequently, could you call me on the telephone or use our social media connection."

OR

> "I know that it is important for you to debrief about George (*the oppressive boss*) when you get home each day. He must have a miserable, lonely work-life. I wonder what sort of pressures he is under. The amount of time we talk about him it seems like George has become an invisible presence in our home. Let's work out a way to limit his influence on us at home so we can enjoy our time together."

Depending on how amicable the separation of a previous intimate

> *A partner from a previous relationship can emerge as a difficult and highly damaging interference*

relationship unfolded, a partner from a previous relationship can emerge as a difficult and highly damaging interference as you embark upon establishing and maintaining a new relationship, particularly if there are children from the previous relationship. Confusing as this might seem, as well as the partner (The Dumpee) who may have been an unwilling participant in the separation, the partner who initiated the previous separation (The Dumper), may be challenged when they become aware that their previous partner is moving on with their life. Very rarely does an intimate relationship come to an end without all participants feeling some level of emotional pain: hurt, betrayal, disillusionment, mistrust, confusion, frustration and anger, self-doubt, guilt, failure, and the list goes on.

The previous partner from an intimate relationship, so it would seem, may take any opportunity to interfere and undermine the new relationship being established. For example: spreading gossip to attempt to do a character assassination on their previous partner, ignoring and neglecting communications regarding children, denying reasonable requests around property settlements and parenting arrangements, and making allegations of past domestic violence and/or child abuse.

Although these are the actions of a person in emotional pain, unfortunately they are likely to pose a significant threat to the newly developing relationship. With each interference from the previous partner, trust will be put on trial in the new relationship. The partner coming into the new relationship from a previous relationship will be tempted to defend themselves, despite the assurances given by their new partner, and reciprocally, a seed of doubt will be planted in

> *Children from a previous relationship have a natural and understandable need to be deeply attached to their parent and will desire to have their own exclusive relationship with them*

the mind of the new partner, despite the assurances given by the partner coming from the previous relationship.

Managing the interference from a previous partner requires a couple to be extremely diligent in exercising the strategies covered in other sections of this book. In addition, Table 2 on the next page lists a number of other important and recommended responses.

Often I have noticed that a relationship with a previous partner is resolved amicably and each party is relatively free to move on with their lives and development new intimate relationships. However, when there are children involved from the previous relationship, all seems to come unstuck when the previous partner enters into a new relationship for themselves. The former partner's new partner will have their own opinions on the previous relationship and the co-parenting arrangements, as well as carrying their own leftover baggage.

Children from a previous relationship can be delicate to accommodate in your current intimate relationship whilst at the same time keeping the intimacy of your relationship exclusive. Children from a previous relationship have a natural and understandable need to be deeply attached to their parent and will desire to have their own exclusive relationship with them.

TABLE 2

Partner from a Previous Relationship	New Partner
Resist the temptation to defend yourself	Don't collude with any accusations or actions against the previous partner
Be utterly truthful with your new partner – even if it is humbling	Ask every question that is likely to disarm any doubts
Keep your promises, behave honourably, and build up the trust between you and your new partner.	Remember: trust strengthens and fluctuates over time
Use the legal channels available to you to address serious issues and accusations	Be patient. Unless there is substance to the accusations made by the previous partner, the issues will resolve over time
Understand the pain of the previous partner, even if you don't agree with it	
Choose to forgive the previous partner, even if you don't feel like it	
Always speak respectfully of your partner's previous partner, especially around children	

Note 12: *The relationship between the children from a previous relationship and their natural parent is distinct from the relationship the children have with the natural parent together with the new partner.*

Unless the children invite the new partner into the intimacy of their relationship with their natural parent, the strength of intimacy between the children and their natural parent will be greater than the intimacy that they share with their natural parent when he/she is together with the new partner.

This is not to say that the children from a previous relationship don't have any relationship with the new partner. It's merely respecting the deep emotional attachment between the children and their natural parent. Reciprocally, the children from a previous relationship, as it is with the children from a current relationship, are exclusive from the level of intimacy you have as a couple.

It is very unfortunate that some couples, often encouraged by the children, seek to negotiate which, and under what circumstances, does one relationship have priority over the other. This is a false dilemma and if it is recognised early, it can circumvent a tremendous amount of conflict and grief. The two relationships may have mutually exclusive boundaries, but they are not competing for the same quality of intimacy. Yes, they both have a level of intimacy, but the quality of the intimacy is radically different.

To prevent the children from a previous relationship becoming regarded as an unhelpful outside influence into your intimate relationship it is important to distinguish and sanctify the quality of the intimacy between you and your partner. In the privacy of your own conversation, identify what makes your relationship unique and exclusive. Avoid asking yourselves questions about which relationship, yours or that with your children, is more important than the other – this is a misleading question that presupposes a differential that is spawned by the insecurity of those who need it to be answered. Rather than give this question validity, ask instead, what can we do to build the sense of security and confidence in the two (or more) intimate relationships?

Ask instead: what can we do to build the sense of security and confidence in the two (or more) intimate relationships?

This principle also applies to other dependents in your relationship, such as your own children, frail parents or other relatives. Of course, you naturally love these people even during times when they can be most demanding of your time, attention, understanding, good-will, compassion, and other practical resources. Despite how difficult your dependents can be at times, it is important that they are prevented from inflicting damage on your intimate relationship. It is the strength and cohesive love of your intimate relationship that is the foundational support to any dependents. The biggest mistake is for one partner to carry all or the lion's share of responsibility for providing support to the dependent(s). The risks to your intimate relationship include:

1) The supporting partner developing, or is perceived to be developing, a bond with the dependent that overshadows or eclipses the bond between the intimate partners.
2) Stress and exhaustion infiltrating the intimate relationship, both of which are risk factors for all the other threats to your relationship that are identified in this book.
3) The build-up of resentment for both partners.
4) The non-supporting partner looking outside of the intimate relationship to fill missing areas of intimacy.
5) The dependent person taking charge of your relationship.

When supporting a dependent, it needs to be clear and agreed to by both partners that it is the relationship that is supporting the dependent person. It is neither one nor both the individuals who form the relationship – it is the

It needs to be clear and agreed to by both partners that it is the relationship that is supporting the dependent person

relationship itself. This is an important distinction. Even if one partner is spending much more of their time and energy directly supporting the dependent, both need to realise that it is the *partnership* providing the support, and that the non-supporting partner is committed to indirectly assisting in other ways.

Chronic Health Issues

Unlike other types of outside intruders which can in many cases be resolved with some clear communications and the restoration of boundaries, a chronic illness is the type of 'embolus' that is likely to become a permanent lodger in your relationship and will test a couple's resilience and commitment.

A chronic illness has the potential to rob you from experiencing many of the loving activities that most people enjoy and take for granted. Spontaneity is replaced with detailed planning, commitments to others are always tentative with the disclaimer that you may need to cancel at short notice, food preparation becomes more like pharmaceutical science, and often sex has become non-existent.

> *A chronic illness has the potential to rob you from experiencing many of the loving activities that most people enjoy*

Often the love in a relationship that has been invaded by a chronic illness seems out of balance. This is an error of understanding and can lead to intense feelings of guilt and possible fear that one day the partner who is the carer will give up and move on. Love is not to be confused with the mere activities associated with being a carer. If it was then most certainly things would be very lopsided. Love is much, much more, and, although it is personally humbling for the partner with the chronic illness, and they might feel a deep sense of helplessness and not being in control, this does not equate to an imbalance of love in the relationship.

The most important thing for a couple to know is that a chronic illness does not define a person and does not define your relationship. Rather, reconstruct the narrative that describes your relationship to encompass the chronic illness and relegates it to a less significant influence. For example, you might agree that you are much, much more than the illness. As individuals and as a couple you are amazingly beautiful, and you would do well to remind each other of this fact every day and many times a day. Though you would not wish a chronic illness on anyone, in many respects it is due to the illness that you have been able to discover otherwise unfathomable loving qualities within yourselves and have experienced so much more depth in richness in your relationship.

> *A chronic illness does not define a person and does not define your relationship*

Living with a chronic illness is a long-term experience that requires vast amounts of care, humility and patience from both partners. Rather than thinking of these as defensive qualities that you need to develop to battle against the illness, it might be helpful to reframe your view of these as loving qualities spawned from the illness itself.

Case History

At this point I wish I was a poet and could capture a definition of love in words. But alas, no. What I have experienced, however, is visiting a very elderly couple where one partner had severe dementia. She could no longer speak coherently and seemed confused about my presence. Her husband, a highly articulate and educated gentleman, spoke on behalf of them both. As we discussed how they were getting along and what plans we might need to consider for the future, he stated, "Wherever I go, she goes as well. We have gone through many ups and downs, we have suffered together, cried together and laughed together. We are a couple!" I don't know what his wife understood of this statement, but as she looked at him, the sparkle in her eyes and glow on her face, was a priceless picture of love.

Addictions

I would like to give attention to an outside intruder to a relationship which may have been covertly attached to a person prior to entering the relationship or could have developed over time during the relationship. Addictions such as alcohol or other drugs, gambling and pornography pose a particularly deadly risk to a relationship. These 'emboli' can do untold damage to the trust level in a relationship, both at the time it is being first identified/exposed/disclosed and during any episodes thereafter.

As with other outside influences, addictions of this nature serve a purpose in the lives of those who have them. That is, although it might be difficult to understand, these addictive outside influences are important to the person bringing them into the relationship. This does not mean they are not responsible for the 'embolus' nor the damaging impact it has on the relationship. It merely removes any judgements on the morality of the person, identifies that the addiction is important to them, and that it is serving a need – indeed, a very deep and complex need.

An addiction is like having a third person in the relationship

Like other outside influences, an addiction is like having a third person in the relationship. For the partner without the addiction, they will need to weigh up whether they can live as a threesome – themselves, their partner, and the addiction – or if the addictive behaviour belongs in the not negotiable category.

Given the significant risk that an addiction can have on a relationship, it is understandable that the partner of a person with an addiction will assign the addictive behaviour to the not negotiable category when deliberating about the future of their relationship. What tends to happen, however, is that those living with someone with an addiction will want, and possibly need, for the relationship to continue, and will do what they can to support their partner, despite the addiction. Unfortunately, in doing so they inadvertently prop up their partner and undermine the tough reality required by their partner to fully face-up to their individual responsibility. True love for a partner living with an addiction is tough love.

> *True love for a partner living with an addiction is tough love*

For the partner with the addiction, the question they will need to ask themselves is: how important is the addiction to them compared with how important do they regard their relationship with their partner? Assuming both partners choose to prioritise the relationship and elect to manage the addiction 'embolism', it is time to seek professional counselling/therapy.

Ghosts from the Past

The more insidious outside influences on your relationship are the intense emotional and psychological hangovers from each partner's history of previous relationships. Often these manifest as overreactions to everyday matters that have triggered painful memories. Despite both partners being able to recognise their haunting and damaging intrusion into their lives, they are still deemed important to the partner who is finding them difficult to let go. To some people their unconscious emotions and memories triggered by events in the present serve as a hypervigilant protective measure. To others they might rekindle uncomfortable feelings such as guilt, shame or resentments. And yet to others they might be regarded with a sense of the sacred.

> *Feelings of guilt will diminish your capacity for sharing joy with each other and will persistently undermine your attempts to build trust*

Whenever a past violation of trust from a past relationship remains unresolved, feelings of guilt will diminish your capacity for sharing joy with each other and will persistently undermine your attempts to build trust. If there is an identified incident(s) from your past for which you are personally responsible and regretful, it is helpful to discuss this openly with your partner. Rather than trying to wage a defence, humbly talk with your partner about:

- Your responsibility for the violation
- What happened?
- What led up to it?
- What motivated you to do what you did?
- How the incident affected you and others (for better or worse)?
- What would you do differently if a similar situation started to eventuate?

> *Unconscious emotions and memories triggered by events in the present serve as a hypervigilant protective measure*

Discuss any potential future fallout from the violation, any options for reparation, and/or if there is an outstanding apology to be made. Once you have done all you can, together with your partner, perform a small ritual of forgiveness to help bury the incident in the cemetery of the past mistakes.

There are also times when a person experiences crippling false guilt over something for which they were either not responsible or only partially responsible. Often this is fuelled by their distorted perceptions and over-generalisation of the incident(s). As with real guilt, the more false guilt is left to lurk around in the unspoken arena of an intimate relationship, the more it is likely to grow and interfere with the flow of love. It never ceases to amaze me how these huge ghosts from the past shrink in size, importance and intensity once they are out in the open and exposed.

> *Huge ghosts from the past shrink in size, importance and intensity once they are out in the open and exposed*

There is another family of ghosts that probably require a little more 'ghostbusting' effort than guilt – resentment, unforgiveness, and bitterness[8]. These ghosts not only want to steal away your joy and happiness, but they also convince you into believing that you are entitled to have their ugly presence in your life. The true intent of the ghosts of resentment, unforgiveness and bitterness is to destroy you and your relationship.

Start your 'ghostbusting' with a clear determination not to host these ghosts in your life. Many events in your life will trigger them to raise their menacing heads, and each time they do, shut them down:

- Interrupt any automatic and ruminating thoughts, change what you are doing; go for a walk, do some gardening, play some music, go to the gym, anything that will change your focus from

> *Choose to release a person from your anger and let go of your resentment*

---

[8] Someone is quoted as saying "resentment is like drinking a glass of poison and hoping the other person will die.

the events of the past and will reinforce what is positive about yourself and your life now.
- Choose to forgive. This doesn't mean you have to pretend that nothing happened, and everything will be hunky dory for the future. What it does mean is that you choose to release this person from your anger and let go of your resentment.
- Raise yourself above the event/incident/person and seek a higher level meaning for what has happened. If you have a faith, engage in your spiritual practice.
- Consult with a professional counsellor/therapist.

Shame is a ghost that deserves a special mention all on its own. If I could personify shame I would have it with an evil smirking face, rotten green teeth, and a long-crooked finger pointing at me while it tells me about how despicable and wretched I am and, most importantly, if anyone knew what I was really like they would despise me. Shame's key strategy for destroying the well-being of our relationships is to stop us from sharing with others what we consider to be our most unlovable selves from the past, most likely from our childhood.

Dealing with shame requires tremendous bravery for a person to disclose the events from the past that the ghost of shame feeds upon. Yet, as with other

> *Once shame is exposed, the claim it has on defining your identity is rendered powerless*

ghosts, once shame is exposed, the claim it has on defining your identity is rendered powerless. A person feels very vulnerable when they talk about the shame and this may only happen in a setting of very high trust. For some people, speaking with a counsellor/therapist might be the place to start.

A partner hearing of the shame needs to be acutely sensitive not to minimise the importance the disclosure is to the person. They are best to listen patiently, slow to speak or even ask questions, and empathise with the vulnerability their partner is experiencing by speaking about the shame. Put any moral judgements to the side for the time being. You can discuss these and/or any legal implications later.

As challenging as this may appear, emotional and psychological legacies or ghosts from past relationships, as with the other outside influences on a relationship, are separate from the person carrying the legacy. As such, they can be thought of and spoken of in a manner that dissociates them from the person. For example: if a partner has a reactionary withdrawal whenever a conversation about money surfaces, instead of referring to it as, 'your issues with money,' you could rephrase it to, 'this issue with money from your past that wants to stop us from dealing with our budget.' In short, although your and/or your partner's past has the potential to have a powerful influence on your relationship, the past is not who you are, nor is it your partner.

Separating events of the past from the person in the present helps to alleviate some of their associated anxieties and resentments. So recognise them as intruders into your relationship, and it unblocks the flow of communication. When memories threaten to haunt us with psychological and emotional pain, try to disarm the ghost by letting the memories serve you as a reminder of how much you have grown in character and strength since that time. Perhaps even engage in a little gesture of celebration – that will shrink down their attempted accusations.

> *Separating events of the past from the person in present helps to alleviate some of their associated anxieties and resentments*

A Concurrent Intimate Relationship

As previously mentioned, an intimate relationship is generally accepted by each partner as an exclusive one. Notwithstanding, there may be times when a partner becomes infatuated with someone else. This may or may not involve sexual infatuation. For some this is merely a passing whim and there is no concern about breaching any relationship boundaries, and for others it could be an intolerable betrayal – a stab in the heart.

Often it is an uncomfortable gut-feeling that signals to a person that there may be a real or potential breach of a boundary to their intimate relationship. This is the time to commence your communication with your partner. If needed, structure your communication to a) be clear and specific about what is concerning you, and b) minimise the possibility that your concerns will be misunderstood or perceived as a comment about the character of your partner rather than a concern about an intrusion into your relationship. Most likely your partner is aware of the real or potential breach being caused by their concurrent relationship, and the conversation you have will evoke a sense of conviction and discomfort. There is a very high potential for them to become defensive.

Typical defensive comments and behaviours include:

- Minimising the significance of the concurrent relationship.
    - "It was nothing."
    - "I was drunk."
    - "We were just working late on something together."
    - "It was a once-off."
- Projecting fault, blaming and excusing their behaviour as a response to the other partner.
- Claiming to be an innocent victim.

- "They kept pestering me."
        - "They came on to me."
        - "I was seduced."
- Gaslighting and claiming that it is all in your imagination.
- Deflecting the conversation by escalating the tension and getting angry.
- Stonewalling by not being willing to discuss the issue.
- Withdrawing intimacy, including sexual intimacy.
- Threatening:
    - To end your relationship.
    - With domestic violence verbally, physically, sexually, financially, socially, spiritually.

Carefully choose your time and place to have this conversation. Refrain from bringing up the issue if you are already experiencing a moment of tension and conflict due to other unrelated matters. If you are concerned about your safety in having this conversation you need to consider a visible, yet private setting, or arranging a session together with your relationship counsellor/therapist.

Although conversations about real or potential breaches to the boundaries of an intimate relationship can be very uncomfortable, but the benefits they afford are worth every moment of disclosure. These conversations will most likely strengthen the boundaries around your relationship, build your trust, and enrich your love. Alternatively, the cost of not having these conversations as soon as they are needed, can have a far more devasting longer term result. Prolonged doubts

> ***Prolonged doubts and fears are more poisonous to your personal health and your relationship***

and fears are more poisonous to your personal health and your relationship than is a concurrent intimate relationship.

In summary:

- An outside influence can pose a serious threat to a relationship.
- Despite its potential risk, an outside influence will be deemed important to you or your partner.
- It is not necessary to fully understand the reason for importance of an outside influence to you or your partner.
- Don't attempt to invalidate the importance of the outside influence.
- Talk together to clarify the impact of the outside influence on your relationship.
- It may not be possible nor wise to attempt to completely remove the outside influence.
- When discussing an outside influence, refer to it as an entity/person in-and-of itself and refrain from assigned personal ownership to either yourself, your partner or the relationship.
- Strengthen your alliance as a couple and collude to manage the outside influence to minimise its impact on the relationship.
- If your outside influence is a person, work together as a couple to express your empathy and demonstrate your respect for the person, and give them direction on how things need to change.
- Addictions require a commitment to seek professional counselling/therapy.
- Emotional and psychological legacies from the past are insidious influences that need to be managed as separate from the person and intruders into your relationship.
- Suppressed memories and emotions lose their strength and power to influence once they are disclosed in a setting of trust and acceptance.

- Confidently and lovingly address the real and potential breaches to the boundaries of your relationship as soon as they arise.
- Make time to regularly recognise, appreciate and celebrate your growth together.

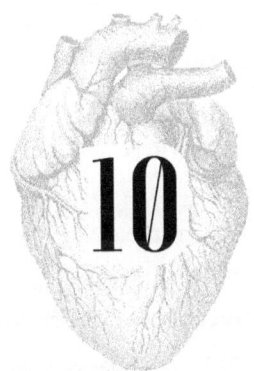

Heart Transplant Donor -Relocating

A heart transplant, or a cardiac transplant, is a surgical procedure to replace a person's heart with a donor's heart. Approximately 85-90% of heart transplant patients are living one year after their surgery, and 75% after three years. One factor that affects the survival rate for a patient who has undergone a heart transplant is the condition of the donor heart - its coronary arteries, the chamber walls, and other damage to the heart muscle.

Whenever someone is asked the question: "Who are you?" or "Tell me about yourself?" they would naturally refer to their name and perhaps to their beliefs, values, strengths and weaknesses and other personal criteria. In addition, they might describe themselves in contextual terms, such as their family, work, where they live, where they might have spent their early years of life, the school they attended, which town or city they are from, etc.

Unless a couple were in the process of relationship counselling/therapy, it would be unusual for them to be asked to describe the internal qualities of their relationship, such as rating their level of intimacy, the quality and effectiveness of their interpersonal communications, their skills of negotiation, and love languages, etc. Likewise, couples may not consciously consider how much their relationship is moulded and supported in the context of their social environment. Although an intimate relationship will have its own distinct identity, inevitably an intimate relationship functions within, and is defined by, a wider set of relationships, norms, rules, laws and expectations from family, friends, colleagues, community, and society generally.

For the most part, as the couple adheres to the behaviour patterns and expectations of their social environment, their social network will serve to support their relationship. They will receive positive responses and reinforcement from those around them and are likely to receive emotional and practical support when stressful issues emerge. If, at times, their behaviour(s) shows any deviation from what is acceptable, they will, overtly or covertly, be encouraged to return to the cultural norm in an endeavour to stabilise the relationship.

In a slow and unchanging world this all sounds quite functional and supportive of your relationship, but alas, in today's society things are rapidly changing around us. Family and friends move on; people lose or change their jobs/careers, and couples, with or without families, are highly mobile and can geographically relocate a number of times throughout their lifetime.

Despite the advent of social media and vastly improved information and communication technologies, as your social network shifts and changes so also does the identity of your relationship. Slow, incremental changes, such as having a close friend move from your hometown to live in another town or city, might be unnoticeable and pose very little risk to your relationship. You might still have many other friends and family living close by, and yes, social media will enable you to stay in regular contact with your friend in their new location. In these occurrences your relationship is likely to maintain its equilibrium or status quo and enjoy the continued support from your social network.

Unlike a heart transplant, which is performed on patients with end-stage heart failure or severe coronary artery disease, a couple may choose to relocate away from their established social network believing that their relationship is healthy and strong. When relocating, however, many of the positive influences that help to maintain and support their relationship and contribute to its stability, cohesion and identity are diminished. For some couples and/or individual partners, this change might be regarded as an opportunity to reinvent themselves, to break the shackles of the expectations of others and venture into new and exciting territory. Other couples might experience this as very challenging and threatening to their relationship. Or it could be a combination of both.

> *When relocating many of the positive influences that help to maintain and support their relationship and contribute to its stability, cohesion and identity are diminished*

Coupled with numerous pragmatic readjustments, such as working out the most efficient transport routes around the community, finding a good General

Practitioner, a school for the kids, the best place to purchase groceries, notifying people and organisations of your changed address, etc, etc, the absences of an established social network can put an intense pressure on a relationship.

Regardless of how well equipped you might be when relocating, without your established social network, your relationship will be vulnerable. When a couple transition their relationship from one social network to another, often any underlying insecurities, unresolved differences and conflicts, communication difficulties, and suppressed hurts manage to find their way to the surface.

> *When a couple transition their relationship from one social network to another, often any underlying insecurities, unresolved differences and conflicts, communication difficulties, and suppressed hurts manage to find their way to the surface*

Like other major upheavals, relocation can be understood and consequently experienced as bringing out the best and/or the worst in our partners. Such an understanding is false, misleading and undermines the endurance and resilience of your relationship. The tensions that arise from relocation are not stemming from either partner's personal weaknesses, inadequacies, and/or moral shortcomings. They are the natural and understandable effects of relocation. Holding yourself and/or each other personally accountable and blaming yourself or your partner for the emotional struggles you and/or they experience as you readjust to your new social environment is not helpful.

Without your well-established social network supporting and defining your relationship, you will need to draw heavily on your negotiation, communication and conflict resolution skills. It will be as if your relationship is reliving the time it first emerged from its romantic inception phase, and you had to renegotiate your differences. You will need to make extra effort to exercise your love languages, structure difficult conversations, defibrillate with some short periods of time-out from each other, temporarily step up the frequency of contact with your remote support networks, and don't be tempted to betray each other's confidence.

Case History

Mikee and Lily had been together for many years. No doubt a little 'Coronary Heart Disease' was setting in and they had lost some interest in the relationship. They were brought up in the town where they got married, attended the local church and by-and-large were emersed in a wholesome family culture. When the opportunity arose to take on a more senior position in a different state, they both agreed it was time for a move. The children were either transitioning into senior school or taking a gap year before going to university. It was after the move that things changed: Mike wanted to be successful in his new role and was spending long hours at work. Lily found solace from her loneliness by spending more and more time with the couple next door who had also recently relocated. She never consumed alcohol at all prior to relocating, but now it helped with her social engagement with the neighbours. It wasn't too long before she found herself spending more time alone and drinking with the man next door – eventually the embolus became an embolism and resulted in the death of the long-term relationship.

> *Relocating is a wonderful opportunity for you to internally strengthen your relationship*

Relocating is a wonderful opportunity for you to internally strengthen your relationship without external props and supports. Unless you work in a highly mobile industry, the experience of relocating may not come around very often and as such it is worth grasping with all your enthusiasm and appreciation. When any underlying issues surface, welcome them as a chance to resolve, heal and build the resilience of your relationship. Get excited and deliberate about building your new social network. Now is the time to join a new interest group, church, sports club, political party, volunteer organisation, study group, and meeting people in your neighbourhood. Although you could benefit from doing these things as individuals, look for things you can do together. Remember your task is to build up a new social network to help support your relationship, not just you as individuals.

Finally, as with a heart transplant, it may take a year or more before you feel comfortably settled into your new community. Yes, there is a possibility of rejection, but relocating into a different community and building up of a new social network is also your opportunity to impart fresh experiences and new energy into the lives of the people you meet and engage with in this community. Persevere with reaching out to others and once they get to know you, the experience will be mutually enriching.

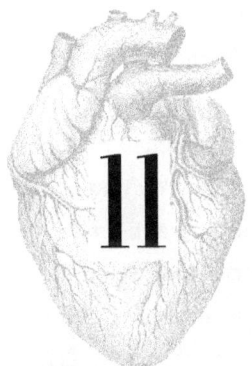

11

Pericarditis – Finances and property

Pericarditis is inflammation of the pericardium, the sac-like membrane that encompasses your heart. When the pericardium becomes swollen and irritated it can cause sharp, stabbing chest pain and abnormal rhythms of your heartbeat. The possible causes of pericarditis include bacterial or viral infection, chest injury, heart surgery and autoimmune diseases.

Few discussions inflame a relationship more than those involving issues of finance. Whether a couple choose to have joint finances, whether they keep individual accounts, or whether one partner assumes a higher level of involvement with the management of the finances, is irrelevant to the tensions they may cause. Money matters wrap themselves around all parts of your life, and unless the dynamics of responsibility for the finances in a relationship are well understood they can cause intense and crippling pain in your relationship.

In a relationship, as it is in life generally, money is a wonderful enabler. It is a convenient medium for making exchanges to help each other satisfy our wants and needs, and it serves a function for storing value for future exchanges. When money becomes an instrument of power and control, however, it undermines and destroys the love in your relationship and is ultimately self-defeating. We will look at this in more detail in Chapter 13 Autoimmune Heart Diseases.

When money becomes an instrument of power and control it undermines and destroys the love in your relationship

In the very early stages of your relationship concerns about money may have seemed petty and inconsequential. If anything, it would have been a simple matter of making sure you or your partner had some cash or a credit card available. Unless you were perhaps an accountant or worked in the finance sector, thoughts and considerations about how this new venture with your partner would impact on your budget would be very low on your worry list. For most couples it was all about the romance.

Notwithstanding, some relationships commence on an unequal financial footing. One partner may enter the relationship with considerably more assets, or more debts, than the other. In the thick of the romance and when you are full of hope and optimism you might set aside any concerns regarding your and your new partner's accumulated assets and/or liabilities

– perhaps you think to yourself that you will cross this bridge later if it ever comes up as an issue. Believe me, it is highly likely that it will eventually rear its head as an issue. Unless you can sensibly and dispassionately resolve significant financial differences, in the heat of a financial conflict, or any other conflict for that matter, the initial financial differential brought into the relationship is likely to be weaponised.

In saying that, perhaps I am being a bit pessimistic and not giving enough credence to the unfathomable self-sacrifice that is involved in establishing and sustaining a healthy intimate relationship. For some couples, despite the magnitude of differences in whatever assets (or liabilities), financial or otherwise, each partner brings into the relationship, when the two become one, both partners agree that they come together as equals despite their differences.

Some people shy away from having a prenuptial agreement believing it somehow diminishes the commitment of one or both parties to the relationship; or some people superstitiously think that a prenuptial agreement pre-empts the demise of the relationship. Where there is a significant difference in the assets and/or liabilities that each partner brings into the relationship, I think a prenuptial agreement is a mature strategy to disarm this ugly beast before it threatens to inflame an already stressful conversation. For starters, a prenuptial agreement does not have to preface itself with "In the event of separation…". A prenuptial agreement is an agreement made prior to marriage that states how you intend to deal with the differential assets and liabilities that you bring into the relationship. For example, it could be written that you agree to merge all the assets and liabilities you bring into the relationship regardless of the differences, or it could be an agreement that you will quarantine your respective assets and liabilities that you have accumulated prior to the relationship and individually take responsibility for such outside of the relationship, or whatever other arrangement you agree on. The point is that your prenuptial agreement does not have to presuppose the possibilities or probability that one day your relationship is going to come to an end. Indeed, the formalised prenuptial agreement could be the very antidote for preserving your relationship as it disempowers the conflict before it begins.

Jump ahead a few years, you may find yourself battling mortgage or rental stress, rising utility costs, fuel and other vehicle costs, school fees, uncertainty with employment, etc, etc, and feelings of being trapped in circumstances beyond your control stealing the joy away from your relationship. You now have the prerequisite conditions for pericarditis and run the risk of not only losing the joy from your relationship, but also finding yourselves increasingly in conflict. During these times, partners are inclined to attempt to restore their sense of control over their circumstances by asserting themselves as individuals.

Left unchecked, individual spending differences tend to intensify. Depending on the social-economic background and family of origin of each partner, where one partner may be more confident and generous in their spending habits, the other may be more conservative. If allowed to escalate these values could become accusations and judgements on each other. Conversations become arguments and words may be used like 'wasting money', 'squandering', or 'careless spending' to describe one partner; and 'tight-fisted', 'miserly' or 'paranoid about money', to describe the other.

Value differences that usually complement each other become sources of tension. One partner may value long term security more highly than short-term fulfilment and when a joint decision is required, partners are tempted to take individual control believing that what they are doing is in the best interest of both partners. Unilateral decisions made by a partner regarding a couple's finances is often the first attempt to take control by an individual. Sure, it might make sense to them based on their individual embedded values, but it is certain to inflame the tension in the relationship.

Effectively managing the financial arrangements within a relationship relies on having a clear understanding that the relationship is an entity separate from the individuals who make up the relationship. Couples may choose to maintain separate financial arrangements (mine and yours). And so long as they have a clear understanding that their relationship also has a separate financial arrangement (ours) for which they have joint responsibility, they can position themselves to prevent financial tensions becoming pathological to the relationship.

Likewise, a couple who choose to fully combine their finances will also have joint responsibility to the finances of the relationship, even if one partner takes a more active role in their day-to-day man-

> *Have a clear understanding that a relationship also has a separate financial arrangement (ours)*

agement. It's common to see in traditional relationships that one partner assumes a greater level of involvement in the management of the relationship's finances. This partner may have more time to give attention to the finances and/or have a higher level of skill or aptitude for financial management. Notwithstanding, the relationship is still regarded as a separate entity from either of the individuals, and still requires joint responsibility. The partner with the more active involvement does not have a mandate to decide and act unilaterally on how the finances of the relationship are managed.

Whether couples choose to keep separate individual accounts and contribute to the joint relationship account, or whether they fully combine their sources of income to have one single account, at some stage(s) it is likely that there will be inequity in the amounts being contributed by each partner. One partner may be on a much higher level of income or indeed might be the sole breadwinner. Resentment might build up for one partner when they believe they are contributing more than their fair share. Reciprocally, guilt and a sense of powerlessness and obligation could arise in a partner who is not able to match the contributions of the other, albeit their non-financial contributions such as childcare, homemaking, and home management may easily match the financial contributions.

Love does not have a monetary value ‖ An important principle to keep in mind is that love does not have a monetary value. How much or how little you contribute to the finances of your relationship is not to be associated with how much value you have on yourself or each other, how much love you have for each other, or how much influence you have in the decisions regarding the finances. For example: if your income is substantially more than your partner's and you contribute much more to the finances of the relationship, or you are the sole breadwinner, this does not privilege you above your partner. Decisions regarding the finances of the relationship are negotiated as equal partners.

As with other negotiations in your relationship, it would be beneficial if you and your partner could come to agreement on any areas of financial decisions regarding your joint finances that can be made alone. That is, you don't want to have to consult with your partner over every little item of expenditure. One of the most basic and yet often neglected processes in a relationship is to work together to formulate an annual budget for your household. Many on-line sites will provide you with a free budget template to guide and prompt you to consider all your income and expenditure. By working together to establish a budget it affords you the time and opportunity to discuss issues of finance before they arise and before they become intensely emotional. It also allows you space to talk about the flexibility you each have in your daily expenditure and what items require further joint discussion.

Unfortunately, we all get stressed and tired, and at times the financial pressures on relationships can seem relentless. The ideal scenario of sitting down with your partner and, in the most mature and loving manner, discussing and resolving important decisions regarding your finances, is simply too difficult and risks only to escalate tensions between yourselves. Consulting a professional financial counsellor offers you the opportunity to step back from the complexity of the issues, which at times can be quite overwhelming. Including a financial counsellor reduces the emotional intensity of the discussion and can provide you with a structured process for negotiating, deliberating, and resolving the next steps in the management of the finances for your relationship.

> *Consulting a professional financial counsellor offers you the opportunity to step back from the complexity of the issues*

It may seem counterintuitive or contradictory to consider spending money consulting with a financial counsellor when most likely your relationship simply doesn't have sufficient funds to pay for everything you currently need. Financial counsellors are only too aware of this dilemma and can also help you with how this can be managed. In most non-government agencies that provide financial counselling the services are subsidised by the government, and it may not be as expensive as you might imagine.

Finally, if it is likely that your intimate partner relationship is ending, the laws relevant to dividing property and finances are complex. It is highly recommended that you seek specialised legal advice (see Chapter 14 – Turning off the Life-Support).

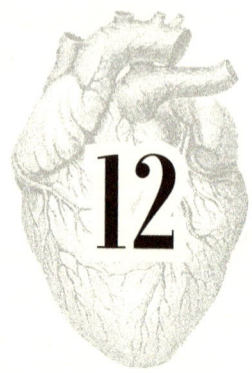

12

Stab wound to the Heart - Betrayal

A stab wound is a penetrating trauma to the heart. While stab wounds are typically known to be caused by knives, they can also be inflicted from broken bottles, screwdrivers, ice picks, garden stakes and other sharp objects. Most stabbings occur because of intentional violence or through self-infliction. A stab wound to the heart is potentially lethal but with appropriate treatment many people survive.

There could be times when those moments of intense emotional conflict involve, to a greater or lesser degree, a violation of one of the non-negotiable areas in your relationship. The feelings evoked could be that of deep hurt and/or betrayal, surfacing as anger, and even rage. Although the types of issues that might be relevant on such occasions will depend upon the beliefs, values, culture and history of an individual, the impact of a violation of trust in an intimate relationship, whether real or perceived, always has the potential to be devastating. Some typical examples of serious breaches of trust include sexual infidelity, unilateral decision making (a decision made by one partner without consultation and/or agreement of the other) on major changes such as relocation due to a career advancement, a significant purchase of a property, car or other item, falling pregnant, having an abortion, the list goes on. What is most relevant is that an agreed, or implied, non-negotiable issue has been violated.

I am going to use the example of *the affair*. That is, it comes to the surface in your relationship, either directly or indirectly, that one partner has engaged in sexual activity with someone outside of your relationship. Firstly, please don't assume by my using this example that affairs are inevitable or are a common occurrence in relationships. I am only using it as an example to un-pack principles for managing significant violations of trust. Secondly, I will be assuming that violation of trust has indeed reached the awareness of each partner. There are various opinions about whether a partner should or shouldn't divulge to their partner any violations of trust that they feel they have committed. Rather than go into the pros and cons of each option, I am going to assume that the breach of trust, has happened, or is happening, and that both partners are now aware of it.

Precisely how the partner who was betrayed came to know about the betrayal is a compounding factor affecting the depth and trauma of the woundedness and the prognosis for healing. On some occasions the betrayal comes to light directly from the perpetrator – the partner who breached the boundary. With genuine contrition they choose their moment to disclose what they have done knowing that the news is going to be deeply hurtful to the other partner and maybe even destroy the relationship.

Much more common is that the partner who was betrayed had their suspicions for some time and the other partner denied and gaslighted until the facts of the betrayal were confirmed and undeniable. Large portions of the perpetrator's time were unaccountable, mysterious texts and phone calls, defensive deflections whenever specific behaviours were raised, and warnings from mutual friends and family, all heralded the truth long before it came into full light. In short, the perpetrator wants to hide from the truth while their partner doesn't want to believe the truth. When the betrayal is finally disclosed, all the previous moments of denial, the lies and deception are as if the knife twists round and round as it penetrates the heart.

On rare occasions the betrayal is intensely traumatic. The partner being betrayed personally experiences the betrayal. They see and/or hear something that can only be compared with significant psychological trauma. They might overhear a conversation between the perpetrator and the other person where the words they overhear burn into their memory like a branding iron. Similarly, when the scenario is visual as when the betrayed partner stumbles upon the perpetrator together with the other person in what is undeniably a breach of the sacred boundary. These stab wounds to the heart are intensely traumatic. The knife not only penetrates, but it also stays deeply and permanently lodged in the heart. No matter how hard they try and how many times the betrayed person chooses to forgive, the memory can't be erased. Indeed, like other intensely traumatic experiences these memories can intrude at unexpected times, haunt your dreams, evoke very hurtful feelings and undermine your self-confidence.

Case History

Neville complained that his partner, Jenny, simply won't let it go. She won't forgive and forget. She keeps bringing up the fact that he had an affair with the wife of a couple that used to be their best friends. She doesn't want to accept his apology and doesn't believe the extra-marital sexual encounter was a one-off event. It was difficult for Neville to accept that he was minimising the extent of his betrayal by focusing on the behavioural event - which may have indeed been a once only. His Jenny, however, was intuitively aware that Neville was fantasising about the sexual encounter long before the physical event. His betrayal happened in his thoughts and imagination months or years before it manifested and he needed to be honest about this. The more he insisted that his betrayal was a once-off encounter and neglected to be transparent about his fantasising, the more deeply he reinforced Jenny's lack of trust in him and confidence in his fidelity in the future.

The most dominant and recognisable feelings associated with a serious breach of trust are likely to be guilt and shame for the perpetrator, and confusion and anger for the aggrieved. Less visible and yet are more penetrating are the feelings which underlie these surface feelings: for the perpetrator they are likely to be feelings of helplessness and loss of control; for the aggrieved they could be feelings of deep hurt, rejection, worthlessness and fear. A stab wound to the heart of your relationship is not a superficial scratch or laceration that can be treated with a salve of reconciling communication and time for healing. Although these

> *A stab wound to the heart of your relationship is not a superficial scratch or laceration*

are necessary, they are rarely sufficient to restore the health of your relationship once there has been a serious breach of trust. Notwithstanding, a stab wound is not always fatal. Healing is possible - yes, it will take time and a great deal of sensitive communication; and, yes there will be a degree of scarring. The surgery required for the treatment of a stab wound begins with, and continues with, a focus on what has been most affected – that is trust.

Healing is possible

Trust in a relationship is not a fixed, rigid commodity. When people say, and believe, that they no longer trust their partner, they run the risk of declaring a self-fulfilling death to their relationship. If you believe that the level of trust in your relationship (yours and/or your partners) has dropped below its level of viability, or reciprocally, that the level of fear in your relationship (yours and/or your partners) has risen above your threshold for safety, then for the sake of all parties, it's time to seek professional relationship counselling/therapy and discuss your options for the future separation.

Trust in a relationship is not a fixed, rigid commodity

When you bear in mind that the level of trust and/or fear in your relationship is not fixed and rigid to every circumstance, and that it is able to raise or lower depending on the situation and behaviours of you and your partner, it might be possible for you to envisage a future shift in your current trust levels that could lead to healing. That is, despite the level of damage done to your relationship through a serious breach of trust, it is possible that both you and your partner may want the relationship to continue and will hold out hope for repair and healing.

To embark upon the pathway to healing requires a willingness from both partners. One partner, understandably the one who has been responsible for the breach, is likely to want to commit

The pathway to healing requires a willingness from both partners

to a pathway of healing much sooner than the partner who is aggrieved. The responsible partner is feeling guilty, powerless and at the mercy of the aggrieved partner. This can be a most difficult and distressing experience, and they may be desperate to return the relationship to a happy equilibrium as quickly as possible. However, even when there is agreement with both partners to work at restoring trust, it is neither wise to attempt a quick fix, nor is it possible.

For the aggrieved partner there is likely to be a heightened sense of ambivalence about deciding whether to work at restoring trust or whether to separate. One moment they might be reminiscing in the memories of happy times from the past, and moments later the events that lead to the hurt and fear overwhelm their thoughts. Although some people might believe they need as-long-as-it-takes to make their decision, and often this can involve time living apart, a prolonged period of ambivalence is neither helpful for their own health or helpful to the relationship. The longer the time a person is caught in this level of ambivalence, the more physically and mentally draining it is likely to become for them, and less likely there will be a restoration of trust in the relationship.

> *The longer the time a person is caught in this level of ambivalence the more physically and mentally draining*

The time it takes for a couple to reach a decision on whether to work on restoring the trust in their relationship or whether to separate is primarily governed by the aggrieved partner. Although it is possible that their ambivalence may dissipate with time and good counselling/therapy (usually not friends and family), the primary

> *Don't be too disheartened, like all relationships, your journey will include occasions where your trust thermometer will rise, and on occasions where it falls*

driver determining the aggrieved partner's timing for a decision is often determined by their belief as to whether the partner responsible for the breach of trust understands the seriousness of their actions, and the likelihood of it recurring.

A decision to work on restoring trust in the relationship is the start of a long, long journey. Don't be too disheartened – like all relationships, your journey will include occasions where your trust thermometer will rise, and occasions where it falls. The aim is to maintain the trust level above your negotiated threshold. Over time the average level of trust in your relationship will hopefully, gradually climb.

A further comment on forgiveness

So much has already been said in this book, and much more could be said about the salving quality of forgiveness in an intimate relationship. Often the people who talk about forgiveness are not people experiencing the hurt and trauma of betrayal, and when they mention the word 'forgiveness' it seems unempathetic, shallow and empty, particularly when the wound is so deep and has been deliberately inflicted on you.

At the risk of being one of those aloof pontificators I would just like to say that forgiveness starts with a vocalised choice: one doesn't wait until one feels better; one doesn't try to clear one's memory; one doesn't wait for retribution; and one doesn't deny that there are consequences that might follow. It's a choice that needs to be vocalised once, twice or a thousand times before you notice any of the above-mentioned changes. The choice to forgive, because it is so counterintuitive, has the additional benefit of reassuring you that you can still experience a sense of self-control. Rather than having unbridled and intense feelings, intrusive thoughts and memories, and the fallout consequences of the betrayal, all dictating life to you, to forgive or not to forgive is entirely in your control.

Table 3 lists a few fundamental actions that can be taken to help raise the trust level in your relationship. All of them involve behaviours that demonstrate trust and none of them rely solely on good intentions, promises and feelings.

TABLE 3

Partner responsible for a breach in trust	Aggrieved partner
• Admit to your responsibility • Reveal only as much or as little of the detail of the incident as your partner is indicating they can cope with. • Don't try to excuse, explain or rationalise your behaviour • Scorch into your memory your feelings of contrition • Apologise for as long as it is necessary • Keep your promises with the little things as well as with the more serious issues • Don't repeat the behaviour or any other behaviour that is likely to be a serious breach of trust • Be patient – very, very patient.	• Listen only to as much of the detail of the incident that you can cope with at any one time. • Don't make excuses for your partner or blame yourself • Be deliberate in your forgiveness • Don't rely on your feelings to determine your forgiveness • Gradually let go of the conversation over the incident – without sweeping it under the carpet. • Increase your awareness of the little things that your partner is being trustworthy with. • Be true to yourself and your thresholds of trust/fear • Be patient – very, very patient

Case History

Robert received a call from a lady he met at a conference who notified him that she had just had his baby. Even before the DNA test showed it to be correct, he confessed to his wife that he had sex with the former colleague. He was deeply ashamed and willing to be fully transparent about what had happened. It became clear that the sexual intercourse was the consummation of weeks of flirting leading up to the conference. He confessed that he thought the flirting was innocent and that he had confidence in where the boundary lay. He said that he thought he could drive his vehicle close to the cliff without going over. He was regretfully wrong. Thereafter, his commitment to his wife was not that he would ever have sex outside the marriage again. His commitment was that he would never drive close to cliffs ever again. Years later a mutual acquaintance said he had met Robert at a barbecue. Robert asked our mutual acquaintance to give me a strange message – he wanted me to know he still avoids driving near cliffs.

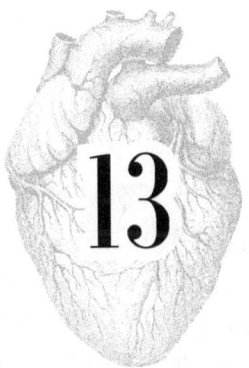

Cardiac (Myocardial) Infarction – The death of a child

Cardiac infarction is commonly known as a heart attack. It occurs when blood flow decreases or stops to a part of the heart, reducing or ceasing the flow of oxygen to the heart muscle. If blood flow is not restored to your heart muscle within 20-40 minutes, irreversible necrosis (death) of the muscle will begin to occur and depending on how much heart muscle is damaged, disability or death can result. Most people (90-95%) of those who make it to hospital will survive a heart attack and the dead heart muscle will eventually be replaced by scar tissue.

The impact that the death of a child, whether they are an infant, teenager or adult, can have on an intimate relationship cannot be overstated. The death of a child is arguably the worst and most severe emotional and psychological pain a person can ever experience. Regardless of the age of the child, parents often feel as if a part of their self has been lost, and their experience of grief is extremely intense and confusing. It is very difficult for a couple to comfort each other when both partners are so deeply grieving. Whether in-synchrony or out-of-synchrony with each other, each parent's mind will oscillate between backward-looking, trying to process what has been lost, and forward-looking, trying to identify how to live in the future without what has been lost.

> *The death of a child is arguably the worst and most severe emotional and psychological pain a person can ever experience*

Some of the more recognised grief responses following death of a child include:

- Emotional trauma and numbness.
- The illusion of expectation: e.g. expecting to see your child in their bed.
- Ruminating and relentless thoughts of what if?
- Indecisiveness.
- Confusion and surrealistic perception – reality and truth become rubbery, and life generally unpredictable.
- Guilt and failure to protect.
- Anger.
- An ache and emptiness in the heart
- Endless reminders and associated sadness.

CARDIAC (MYOCARDIAL) INFARCTION – THE DEATH OF A CHILD

The experience of grief over the loss of any loved one can be intense and heart wrenching. When the loved one is your child, the grief is further complicated by feelings of confusion, injustice and failure. The experience of the death of one's own child is not the way the natural world is supposed to be, it violates the rules of life, and parents struggle endlessly trying to find meaning for why this has happened. For some parents, it shatters their beliefs and understanding of all that makes the world good. Those with a religious faith can feel confused and have relentless thoughts about whether they have been betrayed, abandoned and/or punished by God. A sense of failing to protect their child might also drive them to search for where they went wrong in their parenting. Unfortunately, the search for meaning in a child's death is often unattainable.

The death of one's own child is not the way the natural world is supposed to be

Living through the grief of having lost a child is an individual and unique experience and can last a lifetime. Some people use the language of 'closure' when referring to the journey of grief, as if there is an expectation that one day everything will be put to bed and there will be a return to some form of normality. Such an expectation can exacerbate feelings of guilt and thoughts of "What's wrong with me?" when the ache in your heart forever remains.

The ache in your heart forever remains

Unlike the natural and timely mortality of an elderly person, the losses associated with the death of a child carry forward over the life of the parent. The role of a parent starts with conception and progresses through infancy, childhood and even when their child reaches adulthood. Unless there has been a serious disconnect between a child and their parent(s), parents envisage that they will have an ongoing role in the parenting of their children, sometimes to the annoyance of the children. When a child dies, even in utero, all the anticipated milestones of such as birthing, first solid foods, first words, first steps, starting school, school graduations, engagements, marriage, grandchildren, etc are lost. Around the time these events might have occurred, it can trigger the return of intense feelings of grief.

> *It is not true that most couples separate following the death of a child*

To be very clear, it is not true that most couples separate following the death of a child. Your relationship (heart) has a very good chance of survival. Yes, in some cases the loss of a child can lead to the downfall of the relationship, but just like a heart attack, with timely support you can be optimistic. It is important for both partners to recognise and regularly remind themselves and each other that the pain being felt is due to the loss of a child, not because of anything intrinsically lacking in themselves, their partner, or in the relationship.

> *How, and how long, a person grieves is individual, unique and mostly unpredictable*

There are two people who comprise the heart of your relationship, and no two people grieve alike. Tensions in your relationship following the death of a child are often directly associated with the mistaken assumption that either you or your partner are not grieving the way they ought to grieve. Together with the natural feelings of anger, guilt and often blame that surround the death of a child, erroneous expectations on yourself and/or your partner about how you or they should be grieving will serve only to derail your relationship. The truth is, although there are some generalised responses that people may experience following the death of a child, how, and for how long, a person grieves is individual, unique and mostly unpredictable. For example, merely because the flow of your tears tapered off sooner than your partner does not equate to you being less loving towards your child, and neither does it mean that your partner is wallowing in their lament.

A couple journeying through the loss and grief over a child is also hindered by their ability to comfort and support each other in their times of need and in the intensity of their need. Ideally, as one partner struggles through a bad day the other partner will be doing OK and will be available to support them. This may occasionally happen but certainly should not be expected as the norm. Indeed, the expectations of support each partner has from their partner is often the catalyst for tensions. Mutual support between partners is most desirable and healthy for the relationship, however it is not to be expected.

It is possible that an intimate relationship can strengthen following the death of a child. In keeping with the analogy of the heart, collateral arteries can emerge that bring a quality of life to the relationship that may otherwise not have eventuated. Some areas of personal strengths and character can only be forged in the furnace of very deep pain. To give yourselves every opportunity:

- Be kind and very, very patient with each other.
- Don't be in a rush – take each moment step by step.
- Accept that sadness is a natural part of loss and that it may befriend you for the remainder of your life. Indeed, learn to sanctify and cherish your moments of sadness.
- Give yourselves permission to experience moments of happiness together.
- Mark it in your calendar to celebrate birthdays, anniversaries or other milestones

- Don't attempt to console your partner by saying things like "it's God's will", or "that we'll have another baby", or "at least we have another child".
- Talk with others – join a support group of others who have also experienced the loss of a child.
- Don't leave it too long to consult with a counsellor/therapist, or your General Practitioner (see below).

Source: https://healgrief.org/grieving-the-death-of-a-child/

There is an actual heart condition that is sometimes related to the death of child, or sudden death of a loved one. Takotsubo (pronounced 'tark o soup o') cardiomyopathy or 'Broken Heart Syndrome' is when the heart muscle becomes suddenly stunned or weakened. People with broken heart syndrome may have sudden chest pain or think they're having a heart attack. The condition is temporary, and most people recover within a few months. However, it is very important that if you do experience any chest pain or other physical symptoms following the loss of a child or other loved one that you consult your doctor immediately.

How parents move forward in life following the death of a child is beyond my imagination. Any sense of love, joy and peace they may experience transcends my understanding. Some parents can create their own sacred narrative about the child, which helps them to derive meaning from their loss and a sense of predictability. From the outside looking at such narratives might seems fanciful, delusional and even pathological. It's only the select few parents who have experienced the death of a child can come near to appreciating the power of the sacred narrative.

Case History

Z was five years old and full of energy. He would wake in the morning at top speed and would not slow down until evening when he dropped off to sleep. There were many days when his parents yearned for him to visit his friend's house (my place) so that they could take a break. One afternoon after being asked to remain sitting in the car while his father crossed the road to buy some fruit from a roadside stall Z jumped out of the car and ran in front of passing traffic. He was hit and died instantly. Two days later I met with Z's parents. As I cried in my grief, Z's parents put their arms around me in a group hug. Z's father said, "It's OK mate, Z is now running around in heaven chasing the angels." At first, I was confused by what he said. It didn't match my knowledge of Z's father and the nature of our relationship. At the time we were both headstrong academics at the university. Through my tear-filled eyes I could see that Z's father wasn't simply spruiking off a kindergarten platitude. He was sincerely inviting me to join him and his wife in their sacred, consoling narrative.

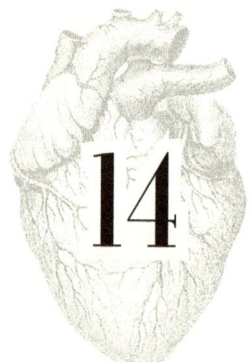

14

Congestive Cardiac Failure – Co-dependency

Congestive cardiac failure (CCF), is a condition in which the heart muscle is weakened and can't pump as well as it usually does. The main pumping chambers of the heart (the ventricles) can change size and thickness, and either can't contract (squeeze) or can't relax (fill) as well as they should. This triggers fluid retention, particularly in the lungs, legs and abdomen.

On the surface the dynamic of co-dependency is quite straightforward and seems mutually supportive. One partner has a need to have someone look after them, and the other partner needs someone to look after. It all sounds quite healthy and balanced, and in a small way all relationships might go through times where we have this kind of need for each other. Where co-dependency emerges is when this dynamic extends to most or all aspects of life within the relationship. Just as the purpose of the heart is to function within the context of the body, so also are healthy relationships part of a wider body of people – a family, a social network, and a community. Metaphorically speaking, co-dependency is like a heart beating away mainly for the purpose of keeping the heart itself alive. The co-dependent relationship is fragile and self-defeating, and involves subtle, and at times blatant, elements of power and control of one partner over the other.

> *Co-dependency is like a heart beating away mainly for the purpose of keeping the heart itself alive*

In healthy relationships it's only natural that partners share a level of dependency on each other. Both partners value the relationship and enjoy supporting each other with their respective needs. They are both confident to express to each other their wants, desires, feelings and needs, and together they find ways to make the relationship beneficial to them both. Although they give priority to their relationship, each partner also has their individual interests and friendships outside of it. They are part of a community individually and as a partnership.

The partners in a co-dependent relationship are very much out of balance. One partner, sometimes referred to as 'the enabler' looks to, and expects, their partner, 'the co-dependent' to meet their every need. The enabler might have a variety of overt and covert, conscious and unconscious, passive and aggressive, strategies to control and maintain the support they expect from their partner. Most of these strategies are contrived to evoke a sense of low self-worth in their partner, and feelings of guilt if their needs are not met and/or the partner prioritises their own needs above those of the enabler. The co-dependent partner will therefore minimise their own needs and make severe sacrifices to support their partner, and to maintain a sense of their own self-worth.

It is a mistake to think that the co-dependent is altogether innocent in this type of relationship. They have a strong need to be needed and will behave in ways to reinforce the dependency of their partner. Their sense of worth and self-esteem is based on meeting the needs of their partner and, like the enabler, they also might devise controlling strategies to keep their partner's dependence upon them.

One of the keys to breaking the dependent-co-dependent cycle is to understand that the relationship is based in fear. Fear is directly opposite to love and will undermine and destroy your relationship. A co-dependent relationship is pervaded by the fears of both the enabler and co-dependent. Those caught deeply in a co-dependent relationship mistakenly convince themselves and others that their fears are expressions of love. Table 3 lists some of the motivating fears lurking deep inside and circulating around a co-dependent relationship and matches them with some of the mistaken beliefs and expressions of love that are often used to mask the fears.

TABLE 3

Underlying Fear	Masquerading beliefs and expression of love
Failure	I love to do my best for you
Abandonment	I love to be only with you
Rejection	I love the way I can help/please you
Upsetting Partner	I love it when you're happy

Making decisions and taking responsibility	I love the way you care for me
Expressing feelings	I love listening to you
Expressing wants and needs	I love to help you
Trusting	I love the way we look out for each other

Ultimately the partners in a co-dependent relationship have a deep fear of intimacy and they are most concerned about their own self-protection from shame. A core belief goes something like: "If you really knew me you would despise me" (see Chapter 7, Cardiac Embolus).

Co-dependent relationships have a deep fear of intimacy

It can be very challenging and anxiety provoking for a partner or couple to resolve to take steps to transform their co-dependency into a more balanced and healthy relationship. Their fears are well founded in past experiences, some possibly from their infancy and early childhood. The risks they would be asking themselves to take are very real to them.

A core belief goes something like: "If you really knew me you would despise me"

Case History

Austen and his partner, Barbara, found each other in their late teens. They each tell a story of how they joked about finding a soulmate who was as socially awkward as they were. In time it became clear that Austen's social awkwardness was a moderate social phobia. That is, he was fearful of being judged and scrutinised by people, particularly in a group setting. Whenever he was invited to a social gathering he would always show up with Barbara. She didn't mind accompanying Austen as she would get anxious whenever he socialised without her and particularly with other women. On the surface they appeared as a beautiful inseparable couple. Behind the public appearances, however, Austen had developed an expectation that Barbara would always give priority to his social agenda and got annoyed with her whenever she had made previous plans. Conversely, Barbara insisted that Austen was never to go to a social event without her and often accused him of being unfaithful. Over time they became more and more socially isolated. They became blinded to their own and their partner's individual qualities, and feelings of resentment regularly dominated their private conversations.

In recognising that you might be in a co-dependent relationship, it is important that you don't add fuel to the fire by condemning yourself further with self-loathing. This is neither truthful, helpful or necessary. Whatever decisions you made along the way to where you find yourselves today were the best decisions you could make at that time.

Start by taking a few very small steps to identify yourselves as individual partners in the relationship. The individuality of the partners in a co-dependent relationship becomes so blurred that they lose sight of who they are separate from each other. It is also important to begin with very small steps like taking a little time-out away from each other each day. Examples might be:

> *Start by taking a few very small steps to identify yourselves as individual partners in the relationship*

- Taking a walk alone for five or ten minutes.
- Calling a friend or family member and chatting for a short while in private.
- Making yourself a cup of tea/coffee and sitting alone for a few minutes.

As you gradually become more confident in your respective individuality, talk together about extending your individual interests and time apart. It might be an opportune time to start a new hobby, join an interest group or a volunteer organisation. That is, without your partner.

More intensive intervention can be made by joining a support group where you can explore your interpersonal dynamics in a safe community, and you can practice expressing your feelings, wants and needs. Individual and/or couple counselling/therapy is also helpful for gaining insights into your embedded, and often unconscious, patterns of responses, and learning ways of reconstructing your thoughts and behaviours.

Most of all, you both need to continue to remind yourselves that it is not helpful for the co-dependent partner to continue to make significant sacrifices to help the enabler.

An intimate relationship thrives when it is interconnected with, and integral to, a wider social network. Just like your heart will be healthiest when it is freely pumping blood around the rest of the body, as well as to itself, so also will your relationship be healthiest when it can focus on the needs of those in your wider social network as well as on the needs of the partners who make up the relationship.

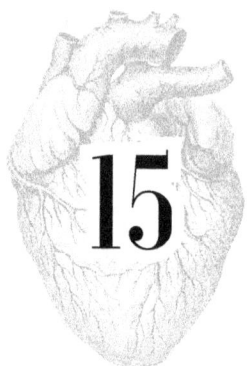

15

Autoimmune Diseases – Self-destroying your relationship

Autoimmune heart diseases are the effects of the body's own immune defence system mistaking cardiac antigens as foreign and attacking them leading to inflammation of the entire heart, or areas of the heart. Autoimmune conditions, in general, occur when the immune system of the body mistakenly attacks its own healthy tissue. The most common form of autoimmune heart disease is rheumatic heart disease or rheumatic fever.

AUTOIMMUNE DISEASES – SELF-DESTROYING YOUR RELATIONSHIP

Autoimmune diseases in the heart of an intimate relationship are the strategies of power and control used by one partner to dominate over the other. That is, your heart is destroying itself.

> *Intimate partner violence refers to violence, abuse and intimidation by one partner over the other person causing fear, physical harm and/or psychological harm*

Intimate partner violence refers to violence, abuse, and intimidation and coercion by one partner over the other person causing emotional, physical and/or psychological harm. In the most obvious cases the abuse is manifested as one partner physically forcing the other partner to comply to their demands, including their sexual demands. Less obvious is verbal, psychological and emotional abuse that does not leave physical scars, but it can have a big impact on a person's mental health and wellbeing. Emotional abuse takes away a person's independence, confidence and self-esteem and can leave them feeling anxious, depressed and even suicidal.

Domestic violence is a betrayal similar to the 'Stab Wound' covered in Chapter 10. The stab wound in domestic violence, however, is deliberately inflicted repeatedly. It's a pattern of chosen behaviour.

<u>Gaslighting</u> is a relatively recent term to describe the subtle, gradual and deceptive undermining of the emotional and psychological confidence of one partner by the other. It is a highly manipulative tactic in which a person, to gain power and control, plants seeds of uncertainty in the thoughts of their

> *Gaslighting is deceptive undermining of the emotional and psychological confidence of one partner*

partner. The partner subjected to gaslighting may start to second-guess what they want, who they are, and eventually doubt their own memory, perceptions of reality, and sanity. The tactics of gaslighting might include: blatant lying, denying factual events, accusing their partner for the faults they experience in themselves, manipulating with a cycle of love and flattery. Also, followed by blame and ridicule, and accusations of their partner being less intelligent, less spiritually enlightened, and/or crazy.

Other forms of intimate partner violence include financial, social and spiritual abuse:

- Financial – one partner taking control over bank accounts and financial transactions and/or forbidding their partner from working or spending their wages.
- Social – isolating someone from their family and friends.
- Spiritual – preventing someone from practicing their religion/beliefs.

The most sinister form of abuse is when both the partner inflicting the abuse and the one being abused have the embedded belief that the abuse is justifiable and appropriate.

For some couples, verbal abuse such as raising their voice and speaking out obscenities at each other is how they have learned to communicate. When one partner feels like they are not being heard or understood they might resort to verbal abuse, which is then returned by their partner. Although there is an element of attempting to control each other, so long as the power differential between the partners is low, the abuse is likely to be contained, and the issues resolved between the partners. However, if there is a significant power differential such as physique, education, financial status and the belief of who is deemed to have ownership over whom, natural conflicts between partners can escalate into intimate partner violence.

Indicators of Intimate Partner Violence

- Subjective fear and attempts at minimisation of conflict.
- Gendered use of power and control.
- Blaming and justification.
- Jealousy and social isolation.
- Arguments that result in one or the other partner leaving.
- Stonewalling or contempt in communication.
- Constant and repetitive arguments that end in leaving.
- Using sexual intimacy for emotional regulation.
- Involvement of children in conflictual patterns.

Source: https://www.psychology.org.au/inpsych/2015/october/weiss

Another way to identify an autoimmune disease infecting an intimate relationship – that is, the hurtful and abusive patterns of behaviour and domestic violence - is to consider the shadow side of the five love languages described in Chapter 5. Each love language can be weaponised against a partner with hurtful, abusive and destructive effect. These behaviours rarely manifest in isolation, but the violation experienced can be more, or less, depending on the primary love language of the recipient. Commonly, the love languages that spoke so loudly during the initial romantic beginning of the relationship later become the means of torment and abuse when an abuser homes-in on their shadow effect:

- 'Gifts', which might have been showered upon a new partner during courtship, later emerge as a powerful and manipulative strategy when a controlling partner restricts the other partner's access and influence of finances.
- 'Words of affirmation' are so beautiful and profoundly seductive at the beginning. When words later become derogatory to, or about,

an intimate partner, they are deeply cutting and wounding to the soul.
- 'Quality time', which is saturated with romance and loving attention during the initial stages of a relationship, becomes abusive when a passive aggressive abuser now chooses to spend most of their recreational time with girlfriends or mates rather than their intimate partner.
- 'Acts of service' – whereas a person may have bent over backwards to support their new partner, but later they inflict their abuse by becoming the king/queen of the castle (the privileged one) and behave in a manner that implies that their partner lives mainly to serve them.
- 'Physical touch' – in the beginning it's the gentle, caressing touch and sexual intimacy – the most intimate of love languages. When physical touch become physical and sexual abuse is potentially deadly, both metaphorically, and literally.

Similarly, 'holes in the heart' described in Chapter 6 can also be identified as strategies for emotion abuse when they are exploited by one partner to hurt, harm and control the other partner. It's as if the abusive partner can sense one or more of the core beliefs or emotional fears listed in Table 1 (Chpt 6) and homes-in on these to attack their partner. For example:

- Fear of abandonment: emotional abuse manifests when an abusive partner is regularly late for appointments with their intimate partner, whereas they don't seem to have an issue with other appointments. Regularly and without notice the abuser comes home late from work, or forgets to attend a special event.

- Fear of failure: an abusive partner will regularly use the word failure in their day-to-day conversations. They might make statements like, "Hey, you failed to buy the such-and-such I asked for"; "You failed to pick up the kids on time"; "You failed to pay the power bill" etc.
- Not good enough: the emotionally abusive partner will regularly make statements to imply that their partner never quite achieved the expected standard. They might make statements like, "This wasn't quite what I was expecting"; "This curry should have more salt"; or more insidiously they might exaggerate the excellence of another person to effectively overshadow their partner.

> *Most intimate partner violence stems from an initial belief held by one or both partners that they are owned or possessed by the other partner*

These and other such behaviours may not mean much in isolated occurrence. When a pattern develops, however, and the behaviours become frequent and regular, they will inevitably have a destructive impact on the intimate relationship.

Often intimate partner violence stems from an initial belief held by one or both partners that they are owned or possessed by the other partner. In everyday language this is usually expressed in conversation as my partner, my spouse, my wife/husband, or I'm his/her partner etc. In most instances this is an everyday common use of language with no abusive intent. For others, the language implies ownership and with it comes an attitude of having claim and control over rights, and expectations for what is deemed to be mine. During moments of conflict, intense emotional stress, financial stress, tiredness, and/or alcohol consumption and other drug misuse, this attitude of ownership manifests in intimate partner violence as one partner seeks to use their power to control the other.

A belief of having ownership of one partner over the other is not necessarily the sole cause of intimate partner violence, nor is it the case that all relationships that subscribe to the ownership narrative/belief results in intimate partner violence. Other causes and contributors of intimate partner violence include a low sense of self-worth by either or both partners, mental illness, personality disorders, prior learning and cultural, religious and gender politics, which include an assumption of male privilege. For some people, the pattern of controlling behaviour they direct towards their partners is not merely a drive to dominate but a pathological fear of not being in control. For them to accept the individuality of their partner and to give them the freedom to exercise their autonomy, evokes intense, uncomfortable feelings of vulnerability and anxiety. Rather than considering the damaging impact their controlling behaviour is having on their partner and their relationship, their foremost concern is to alleviate their own anxieties.

On an even deeper level, the root cause of domestic violence often stems from a deep-seated sense of shame[9] and dysfunctional core beliefs[10] of the abusive partner. For example, a perpetrator may subconsciously harbour a self-identity of 'not being good enough' or has a 'fear of failure'. With a dire need to feel valued and respected, coupled with a fear of one's shame being exposed, a person might resort to using the tactics of power and control, which they may have learned from their role models, or they believe are sanctioned in the realm of gender politics, and/or they believe are their natural or God-given right. Eliciting fear in one's partner becomes a destructive counterfeit for the respect they so desperately desire. Notwithstanding,

---

[9] See Chapter 7 – Cardiac Embolus regarding shame
[10] See Table 1, Chapter 6

this should in no way excuse a person for inflicting abuse and violence against their intimate partner.

Many couples who are experiencing intimate partner violence in their relationships don't want the relationship to end. However, all relationships that involve intimate partner violence in any of its various forms are untenable. The abuse and violence need to stop.

> **The abuse and violence need to stop**

Treating the autoimmune destruction of a relationship due to intimate partner violence requires individual professional counselling/therapy for both partners. Individual counselling/therapy allows the vulnerable partner to speak more openly about the dynamics in the relationship and helps the counsellor/therapist to assess the presence and severity of any controlling or violent behaviours, and any immediate and ongoing safety issues.

First and foremost, both partners need to review whether the relationship is safe to continue, and what needs to happen to ensure the continued safety of the vulnerable partner. A safety plan for the vulnerable partner is mandatory. Ongoing work will require gaining an understanding of the dynamics of power and control, and the cycles of episodic abuse in the relationship; - being honest in recognising behaviours that are abusive, no matter how subtle they might seem, challenging and debunking any beliefs of ownership one partner has over the other, being highly cautious in times of conflict, intense emotional stress, financial stress, tiredness, alcohol consumption and drug misuse, to develop strategies for averting violent and abusive behaviours, and building up repertoire behaviours to increase their own, and each-other's self-worth (see Love Languages).

Couple counselling/therapy is not recommended in the initial assessment of the violence in the partnership, and indeed, depending on the safety and vulnerability of the partner subject to the abuse, and/or the attitude of the violent partner, it may not be recommended, period. There are prerequisite indicators for couple counselling/therapy to go ahead, which can be identified by the counsellor/therapist. These include but are not limited to - the vulnerable partner reporting that she/he feels safe to enter into couples counselling/therapy, the pattern of violence has become less severe and less frequent, the safety of any children in the relationship, and the abusive partner willing to accept full responsibility for their potential to do harm.

> *Some people who have been subject to intimate partner violence come to the point where ending the relationship is inevitable*

Some people who have been subject to intimate partner violence come to the point where ending the relationship is inevitable. The good news is, once someone who was subject to abuse has distanced themselves from their abusive partner, they recover and regain confidence, and the self-worth that they lost when they were subjected to abuse, returns.

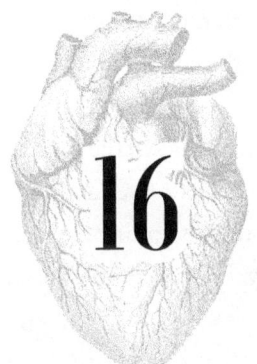

16

Turning off the Life-Support – Ending a relationship

A decision to withdrawing the life support from a patient is a most difficult and heart wrenching decision for the patient's loved ones. Neither is it easy for doctors, nurses, and other critical care staff. Ideally, all members of the care team should be involved in the decision-making process and should have the opportunity to discuss and plan for the aftermath. Patients and families may face difficult ethical, psychological and social barriers as they resolve that the life of the patient is over.

When people enter an intimate relationship, the last thing on their mind is the ending of that relationship. When thoughts of ending the relationship do emerge it is usually followed by a long period of ambivalence. That is, the pros and cons of ending or staying in the relationship can vacillate over-and-over again for weeks, months and even years. Perhaps you have both come face-to-face with the possibility of separation previously, but this time it is different – it's definite.

It is also quite possible that one person has privately deliberated over separation, and indeed come to a decision to end the relationship many months or even years before the other partner. As such, this person is likely to be far better prepared for the aftermath of separation.

Despite some people being ignorant of the condition of their relationship, there are numerous reasons why people stay in an unhealthy relationship or prolong their separation:

- They are likely to have many conflicting emotions that take time to identify, reconcile and prioritise.
- Fear of loneliness.
- They may be concerned about how their social network of friends and family may respond to the separation.
- They may not have a strong social network to support them in the aftermath.
- The care of young children may need to be considered.
- They may have strong cultural or religious beliefs.
- There may be practical deterrents – where to live, separating finances and property, removalist costs, lack of transport, the cost of legal services, etc.

- Mental health and/or psychological strength.

It is worth noting that, although the intimate relationship may be ending, in some cases there will be a continuation of a relationship at some level. The quality and closeness of this relationship will depend upon factors such as the degree of emotional hurt at the time of separation, the emotional maturity of both partners, parenting agreements if children are involved, living arrangements, and other practicalities. The quality of the aftermath relationship is also likely to change over time – generally for the better – emotions will settle, both partners grow to accept the loss, new intimate relationships develop, new social networks develop, and each partner's personal identity is re-established.

Relationship Counselling/Therapy

Just as turning off the life-support to a patient, a decision to end an intimate relationship is best made in consultation with your support team. Preferably, this team would include your relationship counsellor/therapist. Often friends and family are not able to fully understand the complexity of ending a relationship and do not have the skills to identify whether the relationship has the potential for revival. Where it might appear on the surface that a relationship is irreconcilable, a skilful relationship counsellor/therapist may be able to identify reason for hope.

Typical concerns and fears that people have that relationship might be ending are addressed in this book and,

> *A decision to end an intimate relationship is best made in consultation with your support team*

> *A skilful relationship counsellor/therapist may be able to identify reason for hope*

with support from a relationship counsellor/therapist, the strategies suggested might be able to plot a way forward together. For example, people might convince themselves that they can no longer trust their partner. Maybe there has been a 'stab in the heart'. Remember that trust is a fluid commodity. It can rise and fall many times over a lifetime together. If you no longer feel the romance, communications have become difficult, or you are bombarded with financial stressors and other outside demands and influences, these things can be worked through.

It is extremely difficult for people to make sensible, rational and practical decisions, which are in their best interest when their emotions are raw and overwhelming. If the news of the separation comes suddenly to one partner, they could be paralysed by the intensity of the emotions and yet still be required to make decisions that have significant consequences.

Whether ending the relationship commenced sometime in the past or came on suddenly, some of the difficult and intense emotions that partners might need to settle within themselves include:

- Uncertainty, fear and anxiety concerning the future.
- Shame and embarrassment.
- Low self-esteem.
- Residual love for their partner.
- Confusion.
- Hurt.
- Anger.

Feelings are very fickle and can lead you down a pathway of pain and regret

It should be noted that deliberations of ending a relationship based solely on feelings is fraught with danger. Feelings are very fickle and can lead you down a pathway of pain and regret. Notwithstanding, if you are fearful due to a significant risk to your (or your children's) safety (see section on autoimmune diseases), or over time, you and/or your partner feel outright indifferent about the relationship, then the hope for reviving the relationship is extremely low.

Specialised Legal Advice

In an ideal situation, the decision to end an intimate relationship would be mutually discussed and determined by both partners, but this is rarely the case. More often there is a 'dumper' and a 'dumpee', and sadly the idiom of 'do unto others as you would have them do unto you' soon becomes 'do unto others before they do unto you'. The intimacy of love that once dominated the relationship transforms into intense anger, fear or object indifference to the needs of the other. Former partners might behave in ways that are barely recognisable to each other or to themselves. Words like 'we' and 'us' are replaced with 'yours' and 'mine'. Parenting arrangements, property ownership and finances become the battlegrounds for self-interest.

Nevertheless, there are some people who seem to take very little interest in the material assets and practicalities during a separation, and all but surrender to whatever offers are put to them by their former partner. This may be a last-ditch effort to bargain with their partner to reconsider the separation, or it may be a form of passive aggression and abdication of responsibility, and/or the shock, confusion, complexity, and the emotional turmoil of separation is so overwhelming they have very little reserve capacity to make informed decisions.

Seeking specialised legal advice as early as possible is highly recommended. This needs to happen as early as possible in the separation process to ensure that you are aware of your full legal rights and responsibilities, to ensure the correct process is followed, and that you are prepared for making well-informed decisions.

Although seeking specialised legal advice tends to happen following a separation, consulting a Family Law practitioner prior to a relationship ending does not necessarily equate to a final nail in the coffin for the relationship. Indeed, in some jurisdictions a Family Lawyer is required to refer a couple for relationship counselling if there is any possibility for the relationship to recover.

> *Consulting a Family Law practitioner prior to a relationship ending does not necessarily equate to a final nail in the coffin for the relationship*

When seeking specialised legal advice, you are likely to be asked to consider two key areas: Firstly, if there are children involved, what will be the co-parenting arrangements? and 2) How assets and liabilities associated with the relationship are to be divided?– property settlement.

Co-parenting Arrangements

Establishing a co-parenting plan involves creating a written agreement that outlines how parents will share responsibilities and time with their children after separation. This plan should to promote stability and minimize conflict for the children. Understandably parents will have pragmatic limitations such as, work commitments, accommodation capacity, finances etc. which need to be considered, however, it is crucial that the child/ren's best interest remain the primary focus when developing a parenting plan.

> *It is crucial that the child/ren's best interest remain the primary focus when developing a parenting plan*

The best interest of the children may need to take into account things such as:

- The weekly/fortnightly roster of care for the children
- Child support – the financial costs for rearing the child/ren
- Any safety issues, such as domestic and family violence
- Residential locations and travelling needs – consider how far the child/ren must travel between hoes and schools to minimise disruption to their routines
- On-going communication guidelines and boundaries for discussing co-parenting matters

The following questions may help to focus separated parents into establishing a comprehensive parenting plan:

Parental Responsibility: How are the responsibilities for major long-term issues about the care, welfare and development of the child/ren to be shared or delegated between the parents? For example:

a. Education including choice and schools;
b. Religious observance;
c. Significant health care, medical and dental issues;
d. Sporting, cultural and social activities; and
e. Overseas travel including the obtaining of a Passport.

Living Arrangements: What living arrangements (time spend in the are of each parent) can we agree on that would allow the child/ren to have a safe and meaningful relationship with both parents?

> Week Days and Weekends?
> School Holidays?

Father's Day? Mother's Day?
Christmas?
Easter?
Child/ren's Birthdays?
Parent's Birthdays?
Occasional significant/important events?
Changeover arrangements?
Notice time for flexible variations?

Communication with the Child/ren: What is the best way for us to communicate with the child/ren when they are in the care of the other parent? For example:

Telephone?
Facetime
Messenger
Text?
Email?
Scheduled days and times or all reasonable times?

Communication between Parents: As co-parents, what is the best way for us to communicate with each other regarding parenting matters concerning the child/ren? For example:

Etiquette?
In-person?
Telephone?
Text?
Email?
Co-parenting App?
Response times

Education: What areas of the child/ren's education do we need to clarify and agree upon? For example:

> Which school / daycare centre?
> Fees and other costs?
> Extra curricula activities?
> Reports and Attendance at events?

Health, Medical and Dental: What areas of the child/ren's health, medical and dental do we need to clarify and agree upon? For example:

> Which doctor and/or clinic?
> Private health insurance / cost gaps in coverage?
> Emergency contacts?

Financial Support: What financial issues concerning co-parenting of the child/ren do we need to clarify and agree upon? For example:

> Child support payments?
> Extra ordinary expenses
> Process for agree and recouping costs
> Fees and other costs?

Substance Abuse or Misuse: What can we, as co-parents, agree on that will ensure the child/ren are safe from any harm associated with substance abuse or misuse?

Travel: As co-parents, what protocols do we need to agree upon when the child/ren are travelling away from home? For example:

> Taking the child/ren outside of region / interstate / overseas.

Passports
Itinerary and contact details when travelling overseas
Travel insurance for the child/ren
Time limits
Countries being visited

Third Parties : What can we, as co-parents, agree on that will ensure the child/ren are safe and fell comfortable with third parties? For example:

New partners
Housemates
Other family members / children from other relationships
Challenging Behaviours

Care of the children: What other specific and significant care issues for the child/ren need to be clarified and agreed upon? For example:

Priority to the other parent should a parent not be able to care for the child/ren
Other carers
Behavioural boundaries
Safety issues
Screen time
Dietary and other issues

Changes and Reviewing the Plan: How and when do we want to review this plan for our effectiveness as co-parents in the best interest of the child/ren.

When considering co-parenting arrangements separating/separated parents often get confronted with the question of how much agency they should give to the child/ren in the decision-making process. There is no definitive age or clear-cut answer to this question. It will depend on the emotional and cognitive maturity of the child/ren, and whether both parents believe it would be beneficial to hear how the child/ren are experiencing the separated parenting arrangements. Two things keep in mind, however: 1) children should not bear the burden of responsibility for determining the parenting arrangements; and 2) children identify emotionally and cognitively with both parents – symbolically they are half mum and half dad. So, when you are speaking to the children or if discussing the other parent in the presence of children, refrain from making any disparaging remarks, as the children will experience this as if you are referring to half of themselves.

> *Symbolically [children] are half mum and half dad*

Property Settlement

The core premise of dividing property following separation and the ending of the relationship is to achieve a just and equitable outcome. Rarely do individuals who separate after being involved in an intimate relationship resolve their property division and are "happy" with the outcome. Resolutions are rarely perfect, but they can help people unanchor themselves from each other and move forward in your life.

Key factors that separating and separated individuals needs to consider include:

- The value of the individual and overall assets and debts that belong to the relationship – regardless of which individual has legal ownership;

- Who has contributed what to the relationship, both financially and non-financially
- Any factors which will impact each individual in the foreseeable future, such as the arrangements for children, age, and health/medical issues, and the income of each person.

Property ownership and assets' separation are emotionally and psychologically stressful. Along with negotiating parenting arrangements where young children are involved, the process of property separation, particularly when they include substantial debts, a mortgage, relocation, business arrangements and other complexities, can be highly distressing and can have significant long-term repercussions. 'Doin' it y'self' is not a smart idea.

'Doin' it y'self is not a smart idea

However, whatever method is used to negotiate the practicalities of separation, the biggest and most unhelpful factor involved is the fear, sometimes intense fear, by both parties that the other party will attempt to dominate and control them. When responding to the fear, usually the first line of defence is offence – that is, to get in first and dominate and take control. Of course, this only serves to intensify the fear in the other party – and therefore emotional intensity of the negotiation escalates. A more helpful strategy is for both parties to be mindful of this cyclical dynamic and carefully express all their communications to minimise the risk of arousing the other party's fear of being dominated or controlled.

Despite Paul Simon's claim that, 'There are 50 ways to leave your lover', the truth of the matter is that there are no prescriptive ways that make ending a relationship pain-free. That said, there are a few principles and guides that

There are no prescriptive ways that make ending a relationship pain free

can help to minimise pain, and there are definitely a few processes that, if possible, should be clearly avoided:

- Don't procrastinate and delay disclosing your decision to your partner. Once you have reached your decision organise a time and place to speak to your partner so that you can both have as much time as possible to adjust to the change and discuss any practical arrangements for the separation and plan for the aftermath.
- Don't announce your decision to your partner via email, text or on a social media platform. Show a bit of class and dignity and afford a little dignity to your partner. So long as you feel safe and there is no threat of violence, adopt the mindset of having an adult-to-adult, face-to-face conversation.
- Arrange for enough time to allow yourselves capacity to stabilise from the initial emotional impact. Both the dumper and the dumpee will experience intense feelings when they fully realise that the relationship has ended.
- Don't be cruel. Now is not the time to find the lowest points to kick each other with insulting or spiteful remarks about their sexuality or personality traits

> *Don't be cruel. Now is not the time to find the lowest points to kick each other with insulting or hurtful remarks*

- Refrain for going into detailed explanations and reasons for your decision to separate. Although the dumpee might express their need to make meaning of what is happening, at this time it is likely that their emotions are overwhelming, and they feel a sense of loss of control. No matter what reasons are given at this time, they are unlikely to soothe this emotional upheaval. You might be able to discuss your reasons in detail at a much later time. For now, keep the conversation short and simple: e.g. "I've come to this decision over many weeks (or months) and given it endless hours of thought. I've decided to end my relationship with you. I'm not sure of what the future will hold for me, only that I need to separate myself from this relationship."

- Don't be drawn into arguments, discussing details, or the temptation to try again.

Hopefully, as you worked your way through reading this book, the ending of an intimate relationship can be avoided in many cases if both partners are committed to maintaining the relationship and are prepared to:

a) Take an objective view of the health of their relationship.
b) Devote time and effort to doing something different.
c) Challenge unhelpful beliefs about what constitutes a healthy relationship.
d) Acknowledge and accept your feelings but don't be dictated by them.
e) Seek professional help.

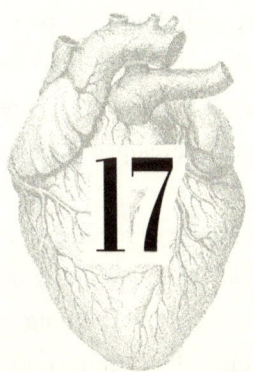

Athlete's Heart – Long-term and mature relationships

Athlete's Heart is a non-pathological condition commonly seen in sports medicine in which the human heart is enlarged, and the resting heart rate is lower than normal. Athlete's heart is common in athletes who routinely exercise more than an hour a day, and occurs primarily in endurance athletes.

It was difficult to resist including a chapter on mature intimate relationships, especially when the metaphor of an athlete's heart came to mind. An athlete's heart is not a pathology as such, but a condition of heart muscle strength that has developed over years of endurance training and performance.

I find it a wonderful reminder of the hope I have for my intimate relationship when I see an elderly couple walking holding hands through the park or along the beach, chatting and laughing together. When launching into an intimate relationship, I think most of us aspire to sharing our full life's journey with our partners – to reach our later years not only to reflect on the meaning of the journey gone, but to also enjoy every new moment with an acute awareness of the pulsating love between us.

Although the issues and strategies of the previous chapters are relevant to all ages, sustaining a healthy intimate relationship into our old age comes with many new and sometimes unique challenges. As an Ol' Mate once commented "You have to be tough to be old."

As ageing creeps up on people, the need to negotiate with their partners might not be so important. Hopefully, the difficult differences between them have been resolved to a satisfactory, if not liveable, landing point. Instead, their negotiation strategies may need to transfer to conversations with their children who, despite what they might choose, will have their own ideas on how they would like their parents to age safely and gracefully. As people grow older, their carer responsibilities might move away from the direct care of their children to their grandchildren who require regular childcare, especially during school vacations. Health issues become chronic and the five love languages are reshaped to accommodate the changes to their physical, psychological and social capacities. For example (jokingly), quality time might take the form of sitting together in the waiting room of the medical clinic, physical touch could be assistance to rise from a chair if their partner has been sitting too long, [11] opening a medication bottle becomes an act of service, a gift might be a new wheelie walker, and words of encouragement might be their partner informing them that their name wasn't included in the obituary list in this morning's news.

Putting aside the flippancy, it is inevitable that the older people get the more losses they are likely to experience[12]:

- Loss of friends.
- Loss of family.
- Loss of fitness, strength and flexibility.
- Loss of health.
- Loss of hearing, sight, smell, taste.
- Loss of mental astuteness.
- Loss of mobility.
- Loss of independence.
- Loss of occupation.
- Loss of worldly identity and social capital – including status, power and authority, work and social relationships, and respect.
- Loss of validating touch points.

As an older person's world contracts from around them, their sense of identity, meaning and purpose can come under threat, or be stripped away. Some folk cope with the transitions associated with ageing by substituting their losses with new activities and new relationships. They might join a senior's group, volunteer at a local service club, start a new hobby, etc. These are great strategies as they also provide a means for allowing a person to continue to contribute to their community.

---

[11] Sexual foreplay might become a game of counting each other's wrinkles.
[12] In my case, a loss of hair – though this went some time ago

Older people might also look towards their partners for their sense of worth and validation. When doing so, some couples could experience an even deeper richness in their intimacy with each other. They might rediscover the lost love languages which, over the years, had become shelved away because of the pragmatism of life. And regrettably for some couples, the short-comings and deficits in their relationship could intensify.

> *Older people might also look towards their partners for their sense of worth and validation*

As more and more of the losses associated with ageing mount up, so also does the opportunity for a couple to move deeper into their love and intimacy with each other. Sadness is a feeling intrinsically connected with the loss of the things we value. The deeper the value of something, or love for someone, the deeper our sadness. It is the shadow cast from love we have for someone who is no longer with us. It's a feeling we reserve for our moments of solitude, or we share only with those most close to us.

The value and importance of companionship intensifies. Sharing your moments of intense grief with your intimate partner is sacred. It immerses you in love. As you mature, both in age and in your relationship, consider each loss and each moment of sadness as the invitation to fall deeper and deeper in love – to further condition your athlete's heart.

> *Sharing your moments of intense grief with your intimate partner is sacred. It immerses you in love.*

A noteworthy loss associated with ageing, which has the potential to evoke feelings of despair and hopelessness rather than sadness, is a loss of one's overall quality of life. Perhaps due to failing health, chronic pain, loss of independence, etc, or due to the cumulation of multiple losses, the quality of life experienced by some folk in ageing is very poor. If the strength of your relationship with your intimate partner is conditional upon your overall quality of life, it could become quite vulnerable when your quality of life retracts, especially in your later years. To resist falling into despair, it is important to focus, not so much on your quality of life, but on your *meaning for life*. It's a focus on how you can continue to contribute to the lives of others. Your love for your intimate partner, or for your children, grandchildren, or your neighbour, is rich in meaning. Few things contribute to lives of others, or are valued more highly, than the love you offer, especially when you have nothing other than your love to give.

> *Focus, not so much on your quality of life, but on your meaning for life.*

End of Life

The love and the life of an intimate partner relationship does not end in the physical death of one of the partners. It is common and healthy for a surviving partner to frequently speak to an intimate partner who has passed away. How a person conceptualises the presence of their deceased partner, what sort of things they talk about, when, where, and how often, depends upon the longevity of their relationship, their level of intimacy, their beliefs and understanding of life after death, and the shared conversations with their partner about dying prior to their passing.

> *It is common and healthy for a surviving partner to frequently speak to an intimate partner who has passed away.*

Understandably, some couples find it uncomfortable to speak openly with each other about the possibility of losing their capacity to make informed decisions, dying and/or how they would like to be remembered and what they believe about life after death. Let's face it, it's not the sort of uplifting conversation you would want to have over breakfast, or lunch, or dinner for that matter. So, when is a good time? Today! Well, perhaps you can at least resolve today a precise time and place to when you will both give priority to commencing these conversations.

Your recommended agenda:

1. **Making a Will**: Both partners need to make a will – a legal document that says what you would like to happen with your money, belongings and other assets (your estate) when you pass away. Regardless of how old you are, don't procrastinate in making your wills. If you have a will, make sure it is up to date.

2. **Establishing an Advance Health Directive:** An Advance Health Directive is a formal way to give instructions about your future health care. It comes into effect only if your cognitive health deteriorates and you become unable to make your own decisions (i.e. lose capacity to make decisions). An Advance Care Directive allows you to: write down your wishes, preferences and instructions for your future health care, end of life, living arrangements, personal matters and/or. appoint one or more Substitute Decision-Makers to make these decisions on your behalf if you are unable to do so in the future.

3. **Enduring Power of Attorney:** An Enduring Power of Attorney is a legal document which can be used to appoint a person to make decisions about personal/health matters and/or property and financial affairs if you lose mental capacity. If you do not have an Enduring Power of Attorney and you lose mental capacity, say with dementia or other related conditions, there may be no one with legal authority to manage your affairs.

How you would like to be remembered: This can be a fun conversation if you choose to make it such. Like, you're not going to be there, right?? It can also be a sacred conversation reserved for only your most intimate moments. Disclosing your inner most thoughts and beliefs, and/or exploring the possibilities about death and life-after-death with your partner is the gateway for the ongoing conversation your surviving partner will have with you after you have passed.

> *The richness of love that is experienced in growing old together is exclusive to those who endure.*

A couple growing old together will have journeyed through a lifetime of joy and adventure, as well as facing countless struggles, conflicts, and moments of suffering. The richness of love that is experienced in growing old together is exclusive to those who endure. It doesn't come cheap and, when it has all been said and done, it is certainly worth it.

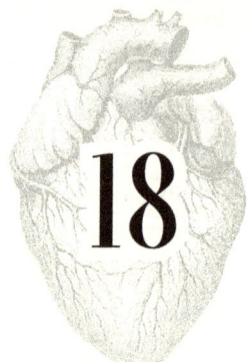

Cardiologist – Relationship counselling/therapy

A cardiologist is a doctor who specialises in the study, diagnosis and/or treatment of heart diseases and heart abnormalities. A cardiologist will carry out diagnostic tests, and perform procedures, such as heart catheterisations, angioplasty, or inserting a pacemaker. A cardiac surgeon may need to open the chest and performs heart surgery.

CARDIOLOGIST – RELATIONSHIP COUNSELLING/THERAPY

Throughout this book I have mentioned the need to see a specialist relationship counsellor/therapist for issues that require intensive intervention and/or if you are concerned that your relationship is coming to the end of its life. Often, when people are seeking medical treatment for the first time from a specialist or from a general practitioner, they ask around to see if anyone knows a doctor whom they can vouch for and has a reputation for being a good doctor. Mainly, people want to know about a doctor's reputation for being competent and has a good bedside manner, that is, that they are effective in their treatments and are respectful to their patients.

As with a medical doctor, it is important to know if the counsellor/therapist you are thinking about making an appointment with is a good counsellor/therapist. Unlike a medical doctor, however, a counsellor/therapist will want to develop a therapeutic relationship with you and your partner where the primary focus is not on your medical condition, nor even on you or your partner as individuals. Their function is to work on the third entity in the room – your relationship. Frequently people enter into counselling/therapy either anticipating that the counsellor/therapist will either help them to fix up their partner – that is, to help their partner understand their issues so that their relationship will mend – or they fear that the counsellor/therapist is going to focus in on their shortcomings and blame them for all the problems in their relationship. Neither is correct, the counsellor/therapist will aim to form an alliance with both you and your partner and together concentrate on this thing called 'your relationship'.

Still, it is important to have confidence in your counsellor/therapist. Let's face it, who would agree to undergoing heart surgery with a backyard novice or a kidney surgeon who was a bit short of work and thought they might just turn their hand to heart surgery for a few days a week? Or what about a heart surgeon who was fully qualified but has a reputation for leaving savage looking scars on a patient's body, or that people frequently died on the operating table? I don't think I would be having them for my doctor, even if they were paid for by the national health system.

Relationship counsellors/therapists come in all sorts of shapes and sizes and practice their trade in a variety of settings. You might hear about therapists such as cognitive-behaviour, emotion-focused, solution-focused, gestalt, psychodynamic, humanistic, attachment-based, narrative, integrative etc, etc. I can tell you the list is as large as the day is long.

The most important thing is whether they can help your relationship

Regardless of what therapy your relationship counsellor/therapist chooses to distinguish themselves by, the most important thing is whether they can help your relationship.

There has been much research conducted on the factors that affect positive change in therapy. Despite the way the theme of this book has been constructed to form an analogy with cardiac conditions and relationship issues, it is a mistake to literally apply a medical model to relationship counselling/therapy. Although there might be some similarities, like exploring your family history and examining your current lifestyle risks, when you consult a relationship counsellor/therapist you are not likely to get a diagnosis and corresponding course of treatments. It will more depend upon the training received by the counsellor/therapist and the therapeutic approaches he/she has adopted that will determine the intervention you will receive. Is one more effective than another? The research says it's not.

What is most important when you first select your counsellor/therapist is whether you believe they can be helpful to your relationship. You might consider the number of letters following their name, a recommendation from a friend, a professional or other person with whom you have confidence, the location of their office, their web-site spiel, the type of vehicle they drive, their gender politics, or other nuanced criteria you might have. If you have a strong belief that they are likely to be helpful to your relationship, you are setting yourself off to a good start.

The real test of whether your counsellor/therapist turns out to be a good counsellor/therapist, that is, good for you in particular, will only come after a number of sessions with the counsellor/therapist, and whether you can notice that they are helping you to achieve the relationship outcome(s) you want. These outcomes will most likely be clarified and negotiated with your counsellor/therapist in the initial session(s). As mentioned above, this may actually mean an amicable dissolving of the relationship. The research of Hubble, Duncan & Miller (1999) suggests that you should notice some level of helpfulness by six sessions with the counsellor/therapist.

From the recommendation from the work of Hubble, et al (1999), ideally your counsellor/therapist will be asking you at the end of each session to rate them with the following scales:

Relationship

| I did not feel heard, understood, and respected. | I————————————————I | I felt heard, understood, and respected. |

Goals and Topics

| We did not work on or talk about what I wanted to work on and talk about. | I————————————————I | We worked on and talked about what I wanted to work on and talk about. |

Approach or Method

| The therapist's approach is not a good fit for me. | I————————————————I | The therapist's approach is a good fit for me. |

Overall

| There was something missing in the session today. | I————————————————I | Overall, today's session was right for me. |

Noting that not every counsellor/therapist uses these scales as a regular part of their practice you might still ask yourself these questions following each session and if you are less than satisfied with how the session went you can mention this at your next session.

Assuming you have been relatively satisfied with each of your sessions with your counsellor/therapist, the proof of the pudding still comes down to how helpful these sessions have been with helping you to achieve the relationship outcomes you want. When you reflect on the outcomes you negotiated with your counsellor/therapist at the commencement of your sessions together, how helpful do you believe your time with the counsellor/therapist has been? Hopefully this will help you to determine whether your counsellor/therapist has been the right person for you. As mentioned above, counsellors/therapists come in a variety of flavours, and merely because one counsellor/therapist has not been overly helpful in your case doesn't necessarily mean that another counsellor/therapist will not be able to meet your needs.

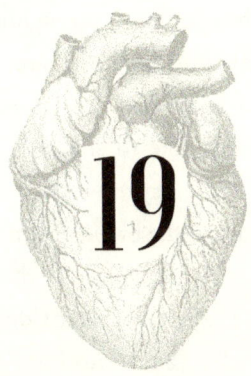

Respiratory System – Replenishing love

The heart is connected to the body's circulatory system by the superior and inferior vena cava, which deliver oxygen-poor blood returning from the body for re-oxygenation, and to the aorta, the major artery leading from the heart to deliver oxygen rich blood around the body.

The heart itself does not re-oxygenate blood. It is also connected by the pulmonary artery and pulmonary vein to the body's respiratory systems. The respiratory system is a series of organs responsible for taking in oxygen and expelling carbon dioxide. As we breathe, the primary organs of the respiratory system, the lungs, exchange these gases in our bloodstream. The oxygen rich red blood cells then travel back to the heart for distribution around the body where it is needed to sustain life.

The metaphor of the heart used throughout this book has assumed that the blood flow into the heart, and through the heart to the other parts of the body, was rich in oxygen from the lungs. As a concluding chapter I would like to stretch the metaphor a little further to explore the source of the oxygen – the source of the love. Oxygen doesn't continuously circulate in the bloodstream as a closed system. As we breathe, a miraculous exchange takes place in the reaches of our lungs. As we exhale, we expel the waste gas, carbon dioxide, which is produced from our metabolism. As we inhale, we take up fresh oxygen from the air into our bloodstream, which circulates to the parts of our bodies to enable our metabolism.

Your relationship is also an open system connected to the world and people around you. As well as love circulating within the heart to maintain its health and function, it also thrives on love being received from, and love given to, others outside the relationship. When the inflow of love to the relationship falls short of what you need to sustain your relationship within, and/or to enjoy the pleasure of giving love to others, you run the risk of developing a self-perpetuating cycle of exhaustion that could eventually lead to negativity, cynicism, and social isolation.

The inflow of love to your relationship can come from many different sources. What is common to each is that, although the love is freely available, it requires you to be open to receive it. Just as the heart has a major blood vessel (pulmonary vein) providing the input, either and/or both partners can be the conduit for receiving love into the relationship. Typical sources of love coming into a relationship could be from children, grandchildren, other family and friends, nature, art and music, literature, and spiritual practice. There may be others not mentioned and those that are particular to yourself.

As an attitude of post-secularism sweeps across the western world, spirituality seems to be regaining credibility and relevance, and people are recognising the importance of spirituality in their own lives and in the dynamics of their relationships. Our spirituality connects us to a love infinitely greater than ourselves.

Given the spiritual nature of love and the fickleness and frailty of people and things of the world, I believe that surest, purest and boundless source of love comes from outside of our worldly systems – namely God.

I am neither a theological scholar nor have I a strong understanding of comparative religion, so I will need to draw upon my own personal faith and leave it up to you to take from it what you deem to be helpful.

From a Christian perspective, God, in Jesus Christ, is both the source of our love and is love itself. To sustain the love in our relationships we need to have a continuous exchange of our worldly selves with the flow of love from God. In each moment as we receive the love of God, it permeates into our individual selves, pours into intimate relationships, and flows through to all our other relationships. It perpetually energises us with what is described in the Christian Bible as the fruit of the Spirit – love, joy, peace, patience, kindness, goodness, faithfulness, gentleness, and self-control.

Just as we have a natural need to breathe to maintain our life and health, we also have a need to continually accept the love of God into our lives to maintain our own health, the health of our intimate relationships, and the health of our relationships with others.

Accepting the love of God into our lives is not a matter of abiding by religious dogma and/or being a good person, it's readily available. Notwithstanding, devoting time each day for spiritual practices such as prayer, meditation and studying scripture helps to facilitate the impartation of God's love. Then, like breathing, throughout our daily lives the love of

God radiates from us without us necessarily being consciously aware or without our deliberate striving.

Better still, as intimate partners, try devoting a set time each day to do something spiritual together. If you can manage to do this you are well-positioned for nurturing, growing and sustaining a strong, healthy and cherished relationship.

> *The love of God radiates from us without us necessarily being consciously aware or without our deliberate striving*

A healthy relationship requires an ample flow of love within and throughout your relationship. The amount of love in your life is not a fixed portion like a deceased estate that needs to be divided up among the potential recipients. Your amount of love rises and falls continuously, *ad infinitum*. That is, there is no limit to how much love is available to you. You are limited only by your willingness to receive that love and then to circulate it both within and outside of your relationship.

Like a healthy heart, you need to be open to receive the love available to you, share it freely between you and your partner, and give it out generously to others.

APPENDIX – LONG DISTANCE RELATIONSHIPS

I have added this appendix for the simple reason that I couldn't come up with a cardiac metaphor that would be analogous to a couple managing a long-distance intimate relationship. Throughout this book I have used the heart as a metaphor for depicting the relationship, with the separate right and left chambers representing the individuals. Stretching this metaphor to describe a long-distance relationship would require you to imagine dissecting the heart and separating the chambers. Of course, this is not a viable, particularly when you would like to be confident that you are able to successfully experience a long-term intimate relationship.

Long-distance relationships eventuate when a couple are required to live far apart and are unable to come together physically for an extended period. It could be for a few days, weeks, months, or perhaps even longer. It could be a single event, continuous or intermittent, such as with fly-in/fly-out workers.

The reasons people choose to be in long-distance relationships vary. It may be an essential component of their work responsibilities, a career advancement, study commitments, visa regulations, family needs, medical treatment, and a host of other possibilities. In most instances, a long-distance relationship is a choice of necessity rather than desire. Whatever the reason, it must be understood that entering into a long-distance relationship arrangement is a mutual decision. You are both in it together even if one partner is located at home while the other is away. You both need to understand and agree to the overall objective of, and the timeframe for the long-distance arrangement.

> *It must be understood that entering into a long-distance relationship arrangement is a mutual decision.*

> *Don't think you can simply 'wing it' when it comes to long-distance relationships.*

Although there are some couples who thrive in a long-distance relationship, for the most part distance does make it more challenging to sustain the health of your relationship and commands additional attention: interpersonal communication is deprived of the nuances afforded by spontaneity and body language; love languages require more creativity and imagination; the integrity of your relationship becomes more vulnerable to outside influences; personal fears and insecurities are magnified, and negotiating differences and dealing with conflict involves even more skill and sensitivity. Whatever you do, don't think you can simply 'wing it' when it comes to long-distance relationships. As well as your deep feelings and

APPENDIX – LONG DISTANCE RELATIONSHIPS

commitment to one another, they require careful planning, coordination and discipline.

All the preventative health strategies and suggestions covered in earlier chapters are applicable for long-distance relationships, though they may require some careful and deliberate massaging. If you are practically able to do so, prior to commencing a long-term arrangement negotiate the expectations you have of yourself and the desires you have for your partner over the things that are important to sustain the relationship. What sort of daily and weekly routines would you like to establish? Are there any non-negotiables that need to be mentioned? Especially discuss how you intend to manage the potential for concurrent intimate relationships emerging. Long-distance relationships are particularly vulnerable to a concurrent intimate relationship developing.

Stay well away from putting yourself at risk of breaching trust

Reaffirm your commitment to fidelity with your partner. Steadfastly resolve with each other to stay well away from putting yourself at risk of breaching trust. As with any time you spend apart from your partner, you would do well to speak and behave as if your partner is alongside of you. If you find yourself considering doing anything that is likely to displease your partner, commit to speaking with them first about it or simply not doing it. You may be tempted to believe you have enough self-control in this regard but far too many relationships come to grief following a cocktail of stress-release, alcohol, and flirtatious behaviour.

During the infancy of living at a distance, quickly get into the preventative health habits described in Chapter 3. These cannot be overemphasised. Greet each other every morning – that's right, EVERY morning. This can be a brief text message or a telephone chat while you are having your breakfast. Mention what you expect to experience in your day, your appointments, tasks, people with whom you might come in contact, etc. Then reconnect at the end of each day or in the evening to keep each other up to date with the events of your day and how they have impacted upon you. From time to time, unexpectedly send your partner a text message or snapshot of something happening during your day. Metaphorically speaking, periodic, spontaneous contact is like giving the health of your relationship a vitamin injection.

Be creative with your love languages. For example:

- Quality Time: could be logging on to watch the same on-line movie together; skype or facetime as you sit in the park or play a virtual board game; or read a part of a book, poetry or devotional material together.
- Words of Affirmation: finish off some of your daily accounts with the words: "Tt was a great day (event/activity). It could only have been improved if you were here with me."
- Acts of Service: many tasks can be completed on-line for your partner – from paying bills, making purchases, researching the best options for products and services, booking accommodation, and planning holidays. Or try doing something special for your partner by proxy. That is, if it's okay with your partner, arrange for a pizza to be delivered to them, or arrange a fortnightly cleaner or someone to do their ironing, contract someone to cut the grass or prune the garden.
- Gifts: a gift that offers tremendous value for low cost is to handwrite a letter to your partner and send it via the regular post. It doesn't have to be an epic novel, even a card or postcard is a powerful way to let your partner know you are thinking of them and that they are special to you.

APPENDIX – LONG DISTANCE RELATIONSHIPS

- Physical touch: it's up to you but I wouldn't advise doing this one by proxy. Instead, use your tone of voice. It can be very intimate indeed, especially if the content of your conversation is, let's say, 'exclusive'.

Long-distance relationships inevitably come to an end at some time. Eventually you will come back together again. For couples who experience intermittent long-distance arrangements, they experience the dynamic of parting and coming back together many times over. They may prepare themselves days or even weeks in advance of each time they part. They spend time talking to each other and reminding themselves about the reason(s) for having the long-distance relationship now in their lives. They reiterate their goals that they hope to achieve, the timeframe and the ground rules. The golden rule is that there should be no surprises in what each other does and how they behave.

When a couple come back together after an extended time apart it can be a little like going on a first date. Again, avoid putting your trust in your intuition to deliver you a positive experience. Make the most of it and plan to do something romantic together.

Regardless of how long you have been apart, or whether this is the first or the 100th time you have been apart, it can still feel a little awkward: like two muddling teenagers. On the upside, it can also be very exciting .

BIBLIOGRAPHY

Anderson, H., & Goolishian, H., 1992, The Client is the Expert: A Not-Knowing Approach to Therapy. In S. McNamee & K.J. Gergen, (eds), *Therapy as Social Construction*. Sage, London.

Beck AT, Rush AJ, Shaw BF, Emery G (1979). Cognitive Therapy of Depression. New York: Guilford Press.

Bowen, M. 1978, *Family Therapy in Clinical Practice.*, NJ: Aronson, Northvale.

Busby, D. (ed) 1996, *The Impact of Violence on the Family. Treatment Approaches for Therapists and Other Professionals*, Ally & Bacon, Boston.

Carter, B. & McGoldrick, M. 1999, *The Expanded Family Life Cycle*, Allyn and Bacon, Boston.

Chapman, G. 2016, *The 5 Love Languages,* Northfield Publishing, Chicago

Corey, G. 1991, *Theory and Practice of Counselling and Psychotherapy,* Brooks/Cole, Pacific Grove.

Dattilia, F.M, 2010, *Cognitive Behaviour Therapy with Couples and Families*, The Gilford Press, New York.

De Shazer, S., 1988, *Clues: Investigating Solutions in Brief Therapy*, Norton, New York.

Egan, G., 1998. *The Skilled Helper* (6th Ed.). Brooks/Cole, Pacific Grove.

Frame, M.W., 2003, *Integrating Religion and Spirituality into Counseling: A Comprehensive Approach*, Brooks/Cole, Pacific Grove, CA.

Fisher, B. 1996, *Rebuilding When Your Relationship Ends*, Impact, California, pp. 272-275.

Freedman, J., & Combs, G. 1996, *Narrative Therapy: The Social Construction of Preferred Realities*. Norton, New York.

Glasser, W. 1998, *Choice Theory*, HarperCollins, New York.

Gilbert, M. & Schumkler, D., 1996, *Brief Therapy with Couples, An Integrative Approach*, Wiley, New York.

Harari, E., 1996, Empathy and the Therapeutic Relationship in Systemic-oriented Therapies: A Historical and Clinical Overview, in C. Flaskas & A. Perlesz (eds) *The Therapeutic Relationship in Systemic Therapy*, Karnac Books, London.

Horne, A. M., 2000, *Family Counselling and Therapy*, 3rd Ed. Peacock, Illinois.

BIBLIOGRAPHY

Hubble, M.A., Duncan, B.L., & Miller, S.D. (eds.) 1999. *The Heart and Soul of Change: What works in Therapy.* Washington, DC, American Psychological Association.

Ivey, A.E., & Ivey, M. B., 1999 Intentional Interviewing and Counselling: Facilitating Client Development in a Multicultural Society (9th ed.) Brooks/Cole, Pacific Grove.

Johnson, R., 2004. Theories of violence and their influence on the practice of counsellingv. *Psychotherapy in Australia.* PsychOz, Carlton North, Vol. 10. No. 4. pp 40- 44.

Johnson, S. 1998, 'Emotionally focused couple therapy' in F.M. Dattilia (ed), Case Studies in Couple and Family Therapy: Systemic and Cognitive Perspectives, Guildford, New York, pp. 450-472

Karen, R. 1998, Attachment in adulthood: The secure base vs the desperate child within, *Becoming Attached: first Relationship and How they Shape our Capacity to Love,* Oxford University Press, New York, pp. 443-445.

McAdams, D.P. 1996, Narrating the Self in Adulthood, in J. Birren, G. Kenyon, Jan-Erik Ruti, J.Schneets & T. Svensson (eds*) Aging & Biography: Explorations in Adult Development,* Springer, New York, pp.131-146.

McKay, M., Fanning, P. & Paleg, K., 1994, Couples Skills, New Harbinger, Oakland CA.

McLeod, J. 1997, Narrative knowing: The nature and function of storytelling in therapy, *Narrative & Psychotherapy,* Chapter 2, pp.28-53.

McNeilly, R.B., 2000 *Healing the Whole Person*, Wiley, New York

Nevels, L.A. & Coche, J.M. 1993, *What Makes Therapy Work? Powerful Wisdom,* Jossey- Bass, San Francisco.

O'Hanlon, W.H., & Weiner-David, M., 1989. *In Search of Solutions: A new Direction in Psychotherapy.* Norton, New York.

Peterson, C. 1996, *Looking Forward Through the Lifespan: Developmental Psychology*, 3rd edn, Prentice Hall, Sydney.

Tracy, D., 2000, Spirit and place, *ReEnchantment: The New Australian Spirituality*, Harper Collins Publishers, Sydney, pp. 111-122.

White, M. & Epston, D. 1990, *Narrative Means to Therapeutic Ends.* Norton, New York.

Worden, M., 2003, *Family Therapy Basics*, Brooks/Cole, Pacific Grove.

www.ingramcontent.com/pod-product-compliance
Lightning Source LLC
Chambersburg PA
CBHW032113090426
42743CB00007B/341